NO ANCIENT WISDOM, NO FOLLOWERS

THE CHALLENGES OF CHINESE AUTHORITARIAN CAPITALISM

JAMES MᶜGREGOR, *1953*

PROSPECTA PRESS

To Jun, Pete, and Quint

Published by

Prospecta Press

P.O. Box 3131

Westport, CT 06880

(203) 454-4454

www.prospectapress.com

Book and cover design by Barbara Aronica-Buck

Print ISBN 978-1-935212-81-2

E-book ISBN: 978-1-935212-82-9

First edition September 2012

Visit http://www.jamesmcgregor-inc.com

for updates and further information.

CONTENTS

INTRODUCTION:
THE FUTURE COMMANDING HEIGHTS   1

The Communist Party of China has two unwavering objectives: make China rich and powerful and guarantee the Party's political monopoly. At the center of this are behemoth state-owned enterprises that dominate all key sectors and have been instrumental to the country's current success. As China's global reach expands, this one-of-a-kind system is challenging the rules and organizations that govern global trade as well as the business plans and strategies of multinationals around the globe. At the same time, the limits of authoritarian capitalism are increasingly evident at home where corruption is endemic, the SOEs are consuming the fruits of reform, and the economic engine is running out of gas. Some top Party leaders are pushing far-reaching reforms that expand the private sector and empower entrepreneurs. But their plans are facing determined opposition from vested interests in the Party that are enriched and protected by the system as it is. The outcome of this struggle is far from certain.

CHAPTER ONE:
STATE ENTERPRISE COMES FULL CIRCLE   13

SOEs are the vanguard of China's authoritarian capitalism. Their history has come full circle. They started as Soviet-inspired drivers of China's industrialization and regimentation under Mao, then faded into the background during Deng Xiaoping's reforms. The SOEs returned to prominence under the Hu Jintao and Wen Jiabao administration as anointed "national champions" to lead China's international ambitions and serve as guarantors of Party supremacy.

PREFACE

China's tenth anniversary as a World Trade Organization member last year sparked the idea for this publication. That milestone provided the opportunity to look back and examine how the Chinese economic system and its interactions with global business and trade have evolved during the country's first WTO decade. That naturally also led to assessing what lies ahead.

My curiosity was partly personal, driven by the various roles I have played in more than twenty years of living in Beijing and by the diverse vantage points those roles afforded me. I started out as the *Wall Street Journal* bureau chief chronicling the resurgence of reform in the early 1990s. After shifting to business as chief executive of Dow Jones in China, I served as chairman of the American Chamber of Commerce (AmCham) in 1996 and as a member of the AmCham board of governors for nearly a decade. Through AmCham and other organizations, I have regularly engaged in policy discussions with US and Chinese government officials. I also journeyed to Washington year after year to lobby for Chinese WTO membership and fair-minded China policies. In researching and writing my 2005 book, *One Billion Customers: Lessons From the Front Lines of Doing Business in China*, I was able to gather insights into many industries and companies and their interactions with regulatory authorities.

This publication is also an outgrowth of a study that I authored in 2010: "China's Drive for Indigenous Innovation—A Web of Industrial Policies." That report examined the Indigenous Innovation policies that China unveiled in 2006 and their widespread repercussions. The report garnered considerable readership because it connected the dots between the Indigenous Innovation mandates and an array of supporting industrial policies that aimed to protect and empower Chinese state-owned enterprises (SOEs) while reducing China market access for foreign companies. Wound tightly into this web were initiatives to foster "national champion" SOEs and state-supported enterprises (SSEs) that can compete globally against the same multinationals that are often forced to partner with these state companies to obtain China market access.

This publication expands on that study by providing a more complex and holistic view of what has become known as the "China Model" and the network of policies that protect and support SOEs, SSEs, and strategic industries. My research team and I found that while they have been beneficial in the past, these policies are increasingly detrimental to China's domestic economic development, international business and trade goals, and its ability to conduct business with and be a trusted partner of foreign multinationals both in China and around the world.

We interviewed many dozens of American, Chinese, and European officials and business people, and pored through hundreds of Chinese and English language news reports, academic studies, and government documents. We drew upon the insightful analysis of China's Twelfth Five-Year Plan by the Development Research Center of the State Council (DRC), and the "China 2030" study the DRC produced in partnership with the World Bank. We also obtained valuable data and perspective from the landmark 2011 study "The Nature, Performance and Reform of State-owned Enterprises" by the Unirule Institute of Economics, an independent Chinese think tank.

We benefited greatly as well from the books *Red Capitalism* by Carl Walter and Fraser Howie, *The Party* by Richard McGregor, and *Bad Samaritans* by Ha-Joon Chang; academic studies by Barry Naughton of the University of California San Diego, Li-Wen Lin and Curtis J. Milhaupt of Columbia University; and a mountain of materials from the Council on Foreign Relations, the Brookings Institution, the US-China Business Council, and the US Information Technology Office, to name just a few.

We also owe a debt of gratitude to the US Chamber of Commerce and APCO Worldwide for their support. The US Chamber provided a seed grant to support the research effort. APCO Worldwide, where I serve as a non-executive senior counselor, allowed me to employ a small team of resourceful and tireless researchers. The research and writing of this publication, however, has been independent of both institutions. The narrative, content choices, editorial judgments, analyses, and opinions are mine alone.

This publication provides a fair but critical examination of Chinese authoritarian capitalism—a system in size and structure that is unique and unlike anything the world has seen. The WTO anniversary is an appropriate trigger for this inquiry, as WTO membership constitutes the first attempt in China's long history to comprehensively integrate into global business and trade governance systems.

Conversations about China in business and government circles today are too often flavored and distorted by propaganda, politics, and the pursuit of profits. In my years of living in China, I have learned that getting the facts on the table is a difficult but important precursor to having constructive discussions. An honest dialogue between the United States and China—involving government and business—is the only way to avoid misunderstandings and conflict. Transparent, efficient, mutually beneficial, and enforceable dispute resolution systems and trade and investment dialogues between the United States and China will be key protectors of global economic prosperity for coming decades. I hope this publication helps clear the way.

James McGregor
Beijing
September 2012

INTRODUCTION

THE FUTURE COMMANDING HEIGHTS

The Russian Embassy in the 1950s was the epicenter of an economic earthquake. Some ten thousand Soviet advisers headquartered in the forty-acre Beijing compound worked hand-in-hand with forty thousand Russian-trained Chinese to industrialize China through central planning and state-owned enterprise. The goal was to overtake Britain in ten years and catch up with America in fifteen.

That fanciful ambition remained elusive, but their "big push" campaign did industrialize and organize the economy. And the Chinese Communist Party (CCP) secured an iron grip on, well, everything: natural resources, raw materials, manufacturing, finished goods, retail distribution, transportation, jobs, housing, food production, health care, communications, imports and exports, and all financial institutions and transactions.

Mao Zedong booted the Russians in 1960, triggering what has turned into a fifty-year quest to infuse the Soviet-inspired system with Chinese characteristics. Mao rescued and regimented the Chinese economy, then spent twenty years ravaging it with his Great Leap Forward, Cultural Revolution, and other machinations. Deng Xiaoping was left with a cadaver of a command economy to resuscitate through market reforms starting in 1978.

Successive Party leaders have mingled various combinations of Marx and the market to create today's unique amalgam that is gaining global recognition as the China Model. Just what is this China Model? China describes it as a socialist market economy. Others lean toward the label "state capitalism." If one examines global economic systems, however, the China Model is most fittingly described as authoritarian capitalism. The ruling Party chooses and appoints the Party members who lead the country's largest and most important businesses, which are almost all state-owned enterprises.

These SOEs monopolize or dominate all significant sectors of the economy and control the entire financial system. Party leaders deploy the SOEs to build and bolster the economy—and undergird the Party's monopoly political control. The private sector provides a lubricant for growth and the opportunity for people to become rich as long as they support the Party.

The current predicament for the Chinese Communist Party is to avoid becoming a victim of its own success. Remaining in power requires continuing to satisfy a restive population that is devoid of ideology and demands nonstop lifestyle improvements. Since Deng launched reforms, China has enjoyed average annual growth of 10 percent. Average per capita income has risen to $4,260* from $180. More than five hundred million people have been lifted above the poverty line. Three years ago, China replaced Japan as the world's second-largest economy, and supplanted Germany to become the second-largest exporter of manufactured goods.[1] China now has more than one million US-dollar millionaires and some 270 US-dollar billionaires.

Party leaders openly admit that this one-of-a-kind Chinese hybrid is in dire need of re-engineering and refueling. Premier Wen Jiabao constantly complains that the economic system is "unstable, unbalanced, uncoordinated, and unsustainable." China's Twelfth Five-Year Plan, launched in 2011, and "China 2030," a 450-page study released in February by the World Bank and the Development Research Center (DRC) of the State Council, essentially calls for retooling the engine, drive train, passenger seating, and navigation system of this Chinese hybrid.

Liu He, deputy director of the DRC, the leadership's top economic advisory body, believes that China can't succeed without resolving four fundamental issues. First, the government must turn its focus to providing services instead of controlling and driving excessive industrial production and GDP growth. Second, the economy needs to shift from exports to domestic consumption. Third, the power of state enterprise and state banks should be reduced as private enterprise and financing mechanisms are expanded to create new waves of consumers. And fourth, the system needs to be restructured in a stable and orderly manner to avoid chaos. In short, the China Model has to morph into a more consumer-oriented, free

* This report will cite RMB or dollars, whichever is more appropriate based on sources and the subject being discussed. When making conversions, the approximate current exchange rate of 6.3 RMB to 1 US dollar will be used.

enterprise, opportunity economy in which the government steps back but the Party maintains its absolute political monopoly.

Liu He acknowledged the difficulties of doing this—and provided a title for this publication—by citing a line from a Tang Dynasty poem: "no ancient wisdom, no followers" (前不见古人，后不见来者). The author was an official who faced enormous challenges as he ventured into uncharted territory. "Policy formulators in China often have a sense of venturing out alone," Liu He writes, "with no ancient wisdom to guide them and nobody appearing to follow them."[2]

A more apt reference may be Mao's 1937 essay "On Contradiction." Mao believed that in some situations a "unity of opposites" can bring balance, and that "contradictions can coexist." But he also warned that if the "groups involved have diametrically opposed concerns" then these "antagonistic contradictions can only be resolved through struggle."

The Russian embassy in Beijing provides a useful starting point for an overview of the struggles, antagonisms, and contradictions this authoritarian capitalism China Model poses for China and the globe.

When it opened in 1658, the embassy sat just inside the northeast corner of the fifty-foot-tall stone wall that encircled the Inner City. The embassy is still there, but the fortification was demolished long ago to make way for what is now the city's Benz-and-Buick-clogged Second Ring Road.

Heading south from the embassy along the eastern section of the ring road is what could be called the National Champion Corridor. Flanking the roadway is an architect's playground of steel-and-glass towers that twist and swirl across the skyline and square-shouldered office buildings that stretch for entire city blocks. These bejeweled and commanding monuments to the China Model belong to a who's who of the state sector. Sinopec, China National Petroleum, China Mobile, Minmetals, China Resources, and the China Poly Group, among others, tower over the Ministry of Foreign Affairs, Ministry of Justice, and other government buildings scattered among them.

These companies are among the 117 central-level SOEs from which the Party is choosing and grooming national champions to go global and conquer foreign markets. Upon these "eldest sons of the republic," as one Party overseer refers to them, have been bestowed a broad range of subsidies, policy favors, protected markets, and even monopolies to arm themselves for their mission of overtaking the world's leading multinationals.

SOEs can take credit for a good part of China's remarkable achievements so far. Without the government's focused planning and formidable ability to finance and execute those plans through state banks and SOEs, progress undoubtedly would have been much slower. In the past decade alone, Chinese SOEs have been responsible for building hundreds of thousands of miles of expressways, city streets, and rural highways; a record-breaking array of bullet trains, railways, and subway systems; and many dozens of ultramodern seaports and expansive airports that are among the world's busiest. At the same time, the government has invested hundreds of billions of dollars through SOEs to reconstruct more than a hundred of China's largest cities—including as much as $50 billion a pop into the metropolises of Beijing, Shanghai, Guangzhou, and Chongqing.

But the SOEs are now consuming the fruits of reform. On paper, these favorite-son SOEs are bulging with profits. But if you take away their subsidies and benefits, the state sector is a big loser. The Unirule Institute of Economics, a respected independent Chinese think tank, in 2011 released a revealing study of the central SOEs as well as their large provincial and municipal SOE brethren. This collection of China's most powerful SOEs reported profits of RMB 5.8 trillion ($920 billion) from 2001 to 2009. Unirule dug up RMB 7.5 trillion ($1.19 trillion) in subsidies and foregone costs, exposing that their real average return on equity in those years was negative 6.29 percent.

Much of this is the result of the Party's course reversal on market reforms with a 2006 directive titled "Guiding Opinions on Promoting the Adjustment of State-Owned Capital and the Restructuring of State-Owned Enterprises." It required a couple of dozen sectors—including telecommunications, power generation, automobiles, aerospace, equipment manufacturing, chemicals, air freight, architecture, steel, and science and technology—to be completely owned or controlled by SOEs. Their coffers were filled when $586 billion in stimulus money mostly flowed into the SOEs in response to the 2008 global financial crisis.

Exact numbers are elusive, but Chinese and foreign analysts estimate that SOEs now account for between 40 and 50 percent of China's current GDP.[3] In the key sectors preserved for the state in the 2006 directive, the

SOEs control between 75 and 100 percent of assets. They also enjoy outsized political influence. Bogged down with project approvals and other administrative matters, government regulators often rely on SOEs—with their large research institutes and massive resources—to draft industrial policies and technical standards. So SOEs often virtually serve as their own regulators.

As Long Yongtu, China's now-retired chief negotiator at the World Trade Organization, put it, "in the past ten years, SOEs, including the state-owned commercial banks, have gained the most from China's reform." Speaking to the Guangzhou-based *Southern Weekly* last year, Long added, "the overall economy has been so good that even pretty stupid SOEs could do well without much effort."[4]

Heading west from the Russian Embassy along the path of the old city wall one passes the golden-tiled roofs and white marble balustrades of the ancient Confucius Temple. It houses stone tablets listing the names of generations of scholars who became officials by passing rigorous exams. Next door is the Imperial Academy, where China's best students prepared for tests by memorizing Confucian classics. The exams engendered unity, continuity, loyalty, and common basic values among officials. They also impeded the development of math, science, experimentation, and discovery, allowing the West to eclipse China in the nineteenth century in what political scientist Samuel Huntington called "The Great Divergence."

The continued quest to catch up was a key motivator for the 2006 Indigenous Innovation campaign that accompanied the reversion to state enterprise. The stated goals were to transform China into a technology powerhouse by 2020 and a global leader in technology by 2050. While calling for fostering open-minded scientists who collaborate with the best scientists across the globe, the Indigenous Innovation plans also directed SOEs to obtain technology from their multinational partners through "co-innovation and re-innovation based on the assimilation of imported technologies." This, not surprisingly, was seen by foreign multinationals and their governments as a blatant blueprint for massive technology theft. The United States, the European Union, and others geared up to find trade-policy remedies. Industrial and technology multinationals strategized on how to remain in China's high-growth market while partnering with SOEs under orders to "master" the foreign technology and beat them overseas.

On the way to Beijing's university district of Haidian, the road passes Deshengmen, the Gate of Virtuous Triumph that imperial soldiers marched through when repelling foreign invaders. When Indigenous Innovation caused an uproar, Premier Wen Jiabao pulled together a team of scientists and technocrats from Haidian and nearby science parks to huddle for a rethink. The loss of trust and goodwill by foreign governments, multinationals, and scientific institutions was bad enough. If China's best scientists were focusing on scrambling for government grants instead of closing the technology gap, then China's hopes of catching the West would remain elusive. Their solution, announced in November 2009, was to focus on "Strategic Emerging Industries" (SEIs). Instead of fumbling around with existing technology, Party leaders decided to leap into the future and focus on next-generation technologies and products. The seriousness of this effort is demonstrated by estimates that as much as $2.2 trillion will be invested in the chosen seven industries—Clean Energy Technology, Next Generation IT, Biotechnology, High-end Equipment Manufacturing, Alternative Energy, New Materials, Clean Energy Vehicles—and in thirty-seven subindustries.

The leadership has a now-or-never attitude toward this initiative. Premier Wen announced the plan to a gathering of China's top scientists with a stern warning that the country had already missed four opportunities for technological modernization since the Industrial Revolution in the mid-1700s. Vice President Xi Jinping, the man designated to become China's top leader this fall, weighed in on the SEIs during a visit to an optical technology research center in Anhui province in April 2011. Xi called for "vigorously cultivating and developing" the SEIs because "they will decide the future commanding heights of the economy."[5]

Though still in its infancy, the SEI initiative appears to be generating the same bureaucratic infighting, SOE favoritism, and focus on extracting funds over exploring science as Indigenous Innovation. Some leading scientists say that only limited progress is possible unless the top-down science system changes.

China's research culture "wastes resources, corrupts the spirit, and stymies innovation," the School of Life Sciences deans at China's top two universities wrote in a scathing September 2010 editorial in *Science* magazine. Peking University's Yi Rao and Tsinghua University's Shi Yigong added, "to obtain major grants in China, it is an open secret that doing good research is not as important as schmoozing with powerful bureaucrats and their favorite experts. This culture even permeates the minds of those who are new returnees from abroad; they quickly adapt to the local environment and perpetuate the unhealthy culture."[6]

The western section of the ring road along the old city wall footprint is now called Finance Street. The road is lined with domestic financial institutions that fuel the China Model, as well as Goldman Sachs, JPMorgan Chase, and other foreign investment banks which help top up SOE treasuries with cash from overseas listings. Located at 25 Finance Street is China Construction Bank, with $1.64 trillion in assets, 313,867 employees, and a 2005 Hong Kong listing that was the world's largest in five years. Just a bit farther south is Industrial and Commercial Bank of China, with $2.04 trillion in assets, 397,339 employees, and in 2006 a $21.9 billion dual-listing in Hong Kong and Shanghai—the world's largest-ever IPO at the time.

They are two of the "Big Four" SOE banks, along with Bank of China and Agricultural Bank of China, that dominate China's financial system and serve as ATMs for the SOEs. In a throwback to the command economy, the government still orders the state banks to provide loans to SOEs and infrastructure projects that are unlikely to be repaid. But the banks are nonetheless guaranteed profitability through fixed interest rates that provide a three-point spread between deposit and loan rates. These policy loans are part of the reason China is breaking world records on the percent of a country's GDP contributed by government spending on fixed investments. Spending on plants, machinery, buildings, and infrastructure now accounts for 48 percent of China's GDP. That is ten points higher than the peak in Japan and South Korea. Most developed countries average 20 percent or less.[7] And the lion's share of this money flows through the SOEs.

This spending binge is leading to a whopping hangover. Corruption is so out of control that the Party is worried about losing its legitimacy. At an event commemorating the Chinese Communist Party's ninetieth anniversary in July 2011, Hu Jintao warned Party leaders about "rampant corruption" with this admonition: "The Party is soberly aware of the gravity and danger of corruption. If not effectively curbed, corruption will cost the Party the trust and support of the people."[8]

A window into the Party aristocracy's use of SOEs to harvest wealth from the system was cracked open by the March detention of Politburo member and Chongqing Party Secretary Bo Xilai for "serious discipline violations," and the arrest of his wife Gu Kailai for allegedly arranging the slaying of a British businessman who was also a family friend over a money dispute.

In the months following Bo's detention, foreign and Chinese reporters dug up public records showing that his elder brother Bo Xiyong is vice chairman (under the pseudonym Li Xueming) of the Hong Kong–traded subsidiary of China Everbright International, an SOE under the Beijing municipal government.[9] Bo Xiyong was also reported to have $18 million in China Everbright stock options. Bo's sister-in-law, Gu Wangjiang, serves on the board of more than twenty companies and owns some $114 million in shares of Tungkong Security Printing Co. The printer's major clients include China's State Administration of Foreign Exchange and the Big Four SOE banks. Tungkong also printed tickets for the Beijing Olympics.[10]

The aftermath of the Bo Xilai scandal illustrates how the Party employs SOEs to maintain stability. Bo and his populist policies were very well liked by Chongqing residents. So less than three months after Vice Premier Zhang Dejiang was dispatched from Beijing to replace Bo, the government announced RMB 350 billion ($50 billion) worth of contracts with several dozen central SOEs to boost the Chongqing economy. This included seventy-two contracts ranging from building power stations, logistics centers, and rail transit projects to creating research centers for car engines and helicopter manufacturing. These SOE investments, framed as a "win-win cooperation" between central SOEs and local businesses, are worth nearly $12,000 per Chongqing resident. [11]

The country's wealth accumulation is reflected in the Party membership shift from its worker-peasant roots to businesspeople and millionaires. Nearly one-quarter of the Party's eighty million members are "enterprise managers or professionals," while workers number seven million. A 2011 study of China's wealthy estimated that the richest seventy members of China's National People's Congress have a combined worth of about $90 billion—and they increased their wealth by $11.5 billion in 2010 alone.[12]

To continue growth for upcoming decades, the Party will have to transform its most downtrodden and exploited citizens—the country's 158 million migrant workers—into full-fledged urban residents and consumers who can fuel the next boom. China's low-cost labor force is shrinking fast. In this decade, low fertility and an increase in years spent in school means the backbone of the factory workforce—those aged twenty to twenty-four—will decline by half, and factory wages are slated to rise by as much as 20 percent annually for at least the next five years. [13] China is also destined to get old before it gets rich. The worker-to-pension ratio is projected to fall from three to one now to one to two in thirty years.

China is now in danger of getting caught in what economists call "the middle-income trap." This can occur when export-led fast-growth through cheap labor and easy technology adoption runs out of steam. To adjust, the economy has to turn to domestic consumption and innovation. But wealthy elites who made money the old-fashioned way usually block reforms. "China 2030" says that of 101 middle-income economies in 1960, only 13 had reached high income status by 2008.

The statistics in support of reform are compelling. Private enterprise and rapid development of the service sector will be crucial to China's continued success. Though blocked from many sectors and largely unable to get bank financing, Chinese private enterprise accounts for 90 percent of new jobs, 65 percent of patented inventions and 80 percent of technological innovation. Meanwhile, Chinese consumption is now only 35 percent of GDP. In the United States it is 71 percent, in Brazil 63 percent, and in India 54 percent. At the same time, only about 38 percent of government spending is earmarked for education, healthcare, and social security—some 16 percentage points lower than countries with comparable income levels. [14]

An eastbound turn off Finance Street at Fuxingmen, the Gate of Revival, puts one on the Avenue of Eternal Peace. This broad boulevard crosses Tiananmen Square under Mao's portrait and passes a multitude of Party and government offices where officials are grappling with the politics and policies of updating the China Model.

Just west of the Zhongnanhai leadership compound is the Central Organization Department's unmarked building. This secretive human resources arm of the Party appoints the officials who fill nearly all important jobs in China. This includes the party secretaries, governors, mayors, ministers, department heads, newspaper editors, television station directors, and university administrators, to name just a few. It also appoints hundreds of the top SOE bosses, and regularly switches them back and forth between government and Party posts. With their enterprises rolling in money, SOE bosses have become Party powerbrokers. They also have the clout to be a formidable obstacle to reform.

Pressures to dial back the influence of SOEs are not only domestic. Trade actions from foreign governments and complaints from multinationals keep officials busy in the gray granite Ministry of Commerce building a couple blocks east of Tiananmen Square. The United States, the European Union, Japan, and other trading partners are working together and separately to devise ways to nullify SOE advantages. This is made more difficult because the waning influence of the United States has weakened the WTO just as the rise of China has become the global trading system's biggest challenge.

Since joining the WTO in 2001, China's share of world trade has nearly tripled to 10 percent. At the same time, with all members having an equal say, the WTO has devolved into a discordant and sometimes dysfunctional democracy. The institution is consequently unable to update crucial accords—embodied in the stalled Doha Round—to effectively address such modern-day trade issues as intellectual property rights protection, cross-border investment, and the manipulation of standards and patents for protectionism. Into this void, China is injecting local practices. When the rules aren't in its favor, China is handling the WTO much like any Sino-foreign joint venture at home. Most prominent is the time-honored technique among SOEs and their government patrons of ignoring the inconvenient parts of written agreements and gaining the upper hand by threatening or rewarding foreign partners to get what the Chinese side wants. "Countries and companies are intimidated against filing cases or even being seen as supportive," said an American trade attorney with long experience in Sino-US disputes. "They are either intimidated or bought off, and usually a combination of those two things."[15]

The Avenue of Eternal Peace meets National Champion Corridor at Jianguomen, the Gate of Nation Building. This intersection marks the western edge of a dazzling cluster of five-star hotels and glass office towers that make up Beijing's central business district. The global financial crisis of 2008 was a game changer for the relationship between China and the world's multinationals that populate this district. The Chinese bureaucracy appeared to conclude that foreigners now need China more than China needs the foreigners. This was evident in the aggressive arm-twisting of foreign companies to hand over their latest technology to Chinese national champion SOEs as the price of market access. The complaints from foreign governments and multinationals led to softened Indigenous Innovation rhetoric and a few policy adjustments. With the more subtle Strategic Emerging Industries initiative, voluntary became the new mandatory. Technology transfer requirements are not put in writing. Instead, verbal requests to "voluntarily" share technology became the market access requirement. "That is the lesson of Indigenous Innovation," said a China-based senior executive of a technology multinational. "Don't write things down clearly. Spread the regulations verbally."[16]

With the Chinese economy sputtering this year, talk of reform has resurfaced. Party leaders in May resurrected a reform package known as the "Thirty-Six Clauses" that was buried by the bureaucracy immediately after being unveiled in February 2005. It outlines what could be the largest opening for the private economy since Deng Xiaoping launched reforms in 1979. Included are ideas for allowing private investment in such SOE citadels as electricity, telecommunications, railway, aviation and oil. Two years earlier, the State Council had tried to revive the package to no avail. Incensed by the bureaucracy's intransigence, Premier Wen this past February demanded that implementing procedures be published in the first half of the year.[17] "Guiding opinions" started popping up two months later. In April, the Ministry of Transport outlined private investment possibilities in transportation infrastructure, services, and related emerging industries. May 2012 brought guidance from a variety of ministries and regulators for private investment in railways, hospitals and clinics, and banks and brokerage firms.[18]

The business community is hopeful but not holding its breath. "Is it a level playing ground?" asked Societe Generale China economist Yao Wei. Speaking to Reuters, Yao said, "You ask private firms for money, but when they go to banks, can they get the same lending terms as state-owned firms? Do they get subsidies like state-owned firms?"[19]

A two-mile ride north along National Champion Corridor from the central business district brings one back to the Russian Embassy. The ideological spat between Mao and Khrushchev that sent the Soviets packing in 1960 is long forgotten. Sino-Russian collaboration these days focuses on such hard-nosed business deals as Russia selling natural resources to China, and China purchasing military technology from Russia. The socialist brothers took different approaches in unwinding their command economies. Soviet SOE assets were scooped up by Party insiders and KGB bosses who are now the moneyed oligarchs.

China opted for a Party-led oligarchy in 2003 by creating the State-Owned Assets Supervision and Administration Commission (SASAC) as the official shareholder of the state's SOE shares. Central SASAC today is located diagonally across the city from the Russian Embassy, just outside the southwest quadrant of the city wall ring road. On paper, SASAC is the world's largest shareholder. In reality, the organization is little more than the SOE secretariat. The Party manages the all-important personnel appointments and significant policy decisions. SASAC is left with little sway to force reforms on independent-minded SOE bosses who can count their profits in the tens of billions and their employees in the millions.

It is no wonder that policy debates and political wrangling about SOE reforms and boosting private enterprise seem to be as circuitous and gridlocked as the ring road route between the Russian Embassy and SASAC. This latest round of reform talk inspired the *People's Daily* to declare that SOEs must remain the "mainstay" as they are "the pace-setters" of technological innovation. The paper warned that foreign multinationals are "striving to control our country's major industries, hoping to become the overlords of some sectors, and only strong state-owned enterprises have the ability to contend with them."[20]

The same argument with a positive spin comes from former SASAC Chairman Li Rongrong, who told reporters in March that SOEs are the superstars that Team China needs to win globally. "Can the Lakers survive without Kobe Bryant?" Chairman Li asked. "Would the Lakers still be the Lakers without Kobe Bryant?"

CHAPTER ONE

STATE ENTERPRISE COMES FULL CIRCLE

SOEs are the vanguard of China's authoritarian capitalism. Their history has come full circle. They started as Soviet-inspired drivers of China's industrialization and regimentation under Mao. They faded into the background during Deng Xiaoping's reforms. The SOEs returned to prominence under the Hu Jintao and Wen Jiabao administration as anointed "national champions" to lead China's international ambitions and serve as guarantors of Party supremacy.

Feeling the Stones

In 1978, the year Larry Bird was drafted by the Boston Celtics and well before China became obsessed with the NBA, Deng Xiaoping inherited a country in deep political, social, and economic turmoil. He decided to use private enterprise to restart China's economic engine.

His strategy was to "cross the river by feeling the stones," allowing experimental reforms to expand nationwide if they proved successful. First came the "household responsibility system" that allowed farmers to market a portion of their crops. Rural entrepreneurs quickly invested their earnings in township and village enterprises (TVEs), small factories nominally connected to local governments that sparked industrial expansion while the SOEs continued to stagnate. In 1978, SOEs accounted for 77 percent of industrial output and TVEs 9 percent. By 1996, the SOE share had shrunk to 33 percent while TVEs had captured 36 percent.[21] Even as GDP growth surged, TVEs claimed an ever-increasing share of the economy, making up 26 percent of the GDP by 1996, compared with 6 percent in 1978. By 1996, TVE employment had grown to 135 million from only 28 million in 1978.[22]

The Shanghai and Shenzhen stock exchanges were formally established in 1990 and 1991. The government decided that the stock markets would be useful to "corporatize" SOEs by selling small stakes to raise money while keeping the bulk of the shares in government hands. Some of the more ambitious SOEs ventured outside mainland China when they discovered that international investors were hungry for Chinese equities. In June 1993, Tsingtao Brewery became the first SOE to list on the Hong Kong Stock Exchange. In 1997, China Mobile Group turbocharged the process with a dual listing in New York and Hong Kong, raising $4.2 billion. Despite these initial capital raising efforts, the SOEs were still a basket case. At its low point in 1997, the entire state sector generated total profits equal to only 0.6 percent of GDP.[23]

These listings were possible because Premier Zhu Rongji placed SOE reform at the top of his agenda. He cleared the way with the 1994 "Company Law" that aimed to transfer decision-making power from the ministries to the new SOE corporate structures. Another turning point in SOE reform occurred the next year, after Jiang Zemin visited South Korea. Chinese planners had been studying Japan's *keiretsu* system, in which individual Japanese companies are linked by cross-shareholdings.[24] But the Korean *chaebols* caught Jiang's eye. The Party felt more comfortable with the Korean model of monopolistic conglomerates backed by government subsidies and preferential financing. At the time of Jiang's visit, the ten biggest *chaebols* controlled some two-thirds of South Korea's economy. Chinese bureaucrats and SOE bosses flocked to South Korea to examine Hyundai, LG Corp., Samsung Group, and other *chaebols*. In the ninth Five-Year Plan (1996–2000), China identified 512 SOEs to be formed into fifty-seven groups.

The Asian financial crisis of 1997–1998 exposed the flaws of the *chaebol* system. Murky financing supporting the *chaebols* helped to trigger that country's financial crisis. Back in China, Zhu Rongji ordered a review of the *chaebol* system, and pushed for Chinese bank reform. The four largest state banks sanitized their books by transferring $480 billion in bad loans to four institutions created to hold the bad debt. The government then recapitalized the four banks and listed them on stock exchanges, raising more than $40 billion from investors salivating for a piece of China's growth.[25]

We Are the Champions

"Grasp the big, let go of the small" (*zhuada fangxiao*) became the rallying cry for SOE reform in 1997. Grasping the big involved reorganizing the largest—typically centrally controlled—firms into enterprise groups under tight state control. Letting go of the small meant that local governments could restructure, privatize, or close down money-losing local firms, many of which had been decimated by competition from the TVEs. The policy left some 117,000 local SOEs to their own fate.[26]

In reforming the SOEs, Jiang and Zhu laid off nearly fifty million workers—some 40 percent of the SOE workforce—over a ten-year period starting in 1993. Local governments took over the sprawling SOE facilities and obligations—their hospitals, schools, sports and entertainment venues, and housing and pension commitments. Large SOEs were separated from their overlord ministries, pumped up with government cash, and repackaged as state-owned corporate structures. The smaller SOEs were sold, or quietly bequeathed, to their managers, government minders, and other well-connected individuals. Workers at centrally controlled urban SOEs dropped from a peak of seventy-six million to twenty-eight million by 2003.[27]

This set the stage for the longtime Party leadership dream of sending the biggest SOEs across the globe as national champions that could compete head-on with the best of the Fortune 500.

The first step was to create SASAC within just a month of President Hu Jintao and Premier Wen Jiabao taking office in 2003. SASAC was designated to be the state shareholder of 196 central SOEs. Local SASACs were established across China to hold the controlling shares of provincial and municipal SOEs. Through a mishmash of reorganization, acquisition, sell-offs, and bankruptcy—often accompanied by very lucrative real estate deals as many of the SOEs were in city centers—the number of SOEs shrank year by year. Central SOEs directly under SASAC's control declined from 196 in 2003 to 153 in 2006, mostly through mergers.[28]

In 2006, Hu and Wen officially turned China back to SOE domination with a directive titled "Guiding Opinion on Promoting the Adjustment of State-Owned Capital and the Reconstruction of State-Owned Enterprises." This drastically expanded China's definition of the state-owned economy by changing key definitions that had been issued in 1999. Most notable was expanding the 1999 description of "industries with a natural monopoly" as suitable for SOE dominance to "major infrastructure and important mineral resources" in the 2006 document.

The circular also designated two categories of industries for heavy state involvement. "Strategic" industries were to be "state dominated" through sole state ownership or absolute state control. This category includes armaments, power generation and distribution, oil and petrochemicals, telecommunications, coal, aerospace, and air freight. "Pillar" industries were to stay largely in state hands, meaning majority state ownership. This category includes equipment manufacturing, automobiles, electronic communications, architecture, steel, nonferrous metals, chemicals, surveying and design, and science and technology.

A package of policies designed to nurture national champions was also released in 2006. Central and local governments were ordered to promote industrial consolidation to build powerful company groups capable of international competition.

One Man Works, One Man Watches, One Man Makes Trouble

"One man works, one man watches, and one man makes trouble." That is how Zhu Rongji defined China's SOEs when he was cleaning up the tattered Soviet-like structures. Though he was joking, Zhu's explanation may constitute the Chinese government's most precise definition of SOEs. The truth of the matter is that Chinese ministries and agencies have a wide variety of definitions for SOEs, and as a result nobody knows exactly how many SOEs exist in China today. Because of this, the SOE share of China's GDP is hard to nail down.

China's National Bureau of Statistics (NBS) itself has a variety of definitions and categories for SOEs. They include SOEs as "non-corporate economic entities, where *all* assets are owned by the state."[29] Another NBS category, "state-holding enterprises," refers to "enterprises where the percentage of state assets (or shares held by the state) is larger than any other single shareholder of the same enterprise."[30] Many academics consider the combination of these two NBS categories to be the official state sector for statistical purposes. It would be nice if things were that simple. NBS considers any company with foreign investment outside the SOE definition and therefore inappropriate to include in the bureau's SOE statistics. Another NBS qualification for SOE designation is that the entity has to be an industrial enterprise and be engaged in such activities as the extraction of natural resources, the processing of minerals and agricultural products, or the manufacturing or repairing of industrial products.[31] The NBS maintains separate categories for enterprises in such sectors as agriculture, construction, transport, post and telecom services, banking, and insurance. Even more confusing are NBS definitions that require enterprises to be above a "designated size" to make it into the bureau's statistical base. In 1996, the threshold was exceeding RMB 500 million in annual sales. In 2006, this was increased to RMB 5 billion. In 2011, it was raised to RMB 20 billion.[32] The government's statisticians obviously decided that it is impossible to keep track of China's smaller companies, be they SOEs, private, or a mixture.

Applying a narrow NBS definition, China officially reported a total of

9,105 state-owned enterprises and 11,405 state-holding enterprises in 2010—or a total of 20,510 SOEs.[33] That same year, former SASAC Chairman Li Rongrong declared that China had 114,500 SOEs.[34]

As to the SOE share of the Chinese economy, the only way to even attempt to calculate that number is to triangulate from various estimates. In 2006, as additional SOE subsidies and preferences were just being launched, the Organization for Economic Co-operation and Development (OECD) estimated SOEs accounted for as low as 30 percent of China's GDP. The US-China Economic and Security Review Commission (USCC) recently estimated that SOEs accounted for 40 percent of GDP in 2007. The USCC suggested it might be a conservative estimate. Today, following a flood of favorable SOE policies and the bulk of China's $586 billion post-financial-crisis stimulus money going into SOE coffers, some economists and analysts estimate that the SOE share of GDP may well exceed 50 percent.[35] Even with its narrow SOE definitions, China's NBS estimates that SOEs account for nearly 30 percent of urban employment, and more than half of total urban wages. Former SASAC Chairman Li recently said that centrally-owned SOEs control more than 90 percent of assets in several of China's strategic and pillar industries.[36] The sectors with the highest SOE participation are telecom (96.2 percent), power (91.6 percent), petroleum and petrochemicals (76.6 percent), air transportation (76.2 percent), and automobiles (74 percent). [37]

What this all adds up to is that SOEs dominate China's major industrial sectors and account for somewhere between 40 percent and 50 percent of GDP.

Red Hats and Corporate Cross-Dressing

Remember the township and village enterprises, or TVEs, that cracked open the private economy? They emerged by the tens of thousands from the communes and collectives to transform themselves into private businesses after the 1994 Company Law. They are known as "red hat" companies because their founders parked themselves under the government in the early reform days when it was still risky to be labeled a capitalist. A 1994 survey by the State Administration of Industry and Commerce found that 83 percent of the collective TVEs were, in practice, private enterprises.[38]

Nonetheless, wearing these government red hats provided such perks as tax breaks and access to state bank credit. Another reason to don a red hat was that private companies were excluded from some thirty industries at that time.[39] In his book *The Party: The Secret World of China's Communist Rulers,* Richard McGregor says that red hats allowed companies to gain the benefits of being simultaneously private and state-owned. "The corporate cross-dressing complicates life for an entrepreneur, but it is common sense as well," McGregor wrote. "The smartest companies have become adept at having it both ways."[40]

A 1989 survey by the Chinese Academy of Social Sciences found that more than one-third of the TVEs in the booming coastal provinces of Jiangsu, Zhejiang, and Guangdong were in fact red hat enterprises. An academy researcher put it this way: "Some made money because they had power. Others gained power because they had money. China's private companies are just as complicated as the SOEs."[41]

These companies with red hat origins continue to muddle official statistics and blur the line between state and private enterprises. "Without the red hat, we wouldn't have been able to develop so fast," Wang Shi, Chairman of Vanke, China's largest residential real estate developer and a former red hat enterprise, told an interviewer in 2008. "They are in every industry."[42]

The Eldest Sons of the Republic

SOEs can be useful for certain industries at certain stages of economic development. This includes circumstances in which markets are not likely to meet the basic needs of poor people—and countries need to industrialize and boost economic growth to escape poverty. The sectors involved often include basic infrastructure, primary health care, education, transportation, and some types of scientific research. These state enterprises are necessary when the private sector is reluctant to commit capital due to high risk and long development horizons. Another motivation is preventing private monopolies over public services which would have excessive pricing power.

Reformers in China in the 1990s were headed toward limiting the SOE sector to "natural monopolies" in such public services as transport, water, and electricity. As the private sector expanded, however, the Party concluded in the mid-2000s that a dominant state sector was necessary for achieving government economic objectives and maintaining the Party's monopoly on political control. The privatization of state assets in Russia by individual oligarchs triggered alarms in the Zhongnanhai leadership compound. As they watched former KGB insiders and other powerful individuals scoop up Russia's natural resources and other valuable state assets, Party leaders in China realized this was also happening on a smaller scale in Chinese provinces and cities. Under the "let go of the small" SOE reforms, Chinese bureaucrats-turned-businessmen were grabbing the best SOE factories, making fortunes from the real estate and becoming kingpins with ample cash to pad the pockets of local Party officials.

To avoid the rise of Russian-style individual oligarchs across China, the Party decided that it should be the oligarchy that controls all of the important and rich SOEs. This was accomplished by teaming SASAC, the designated government shareholder, with the Party's Central Organization Department, which could control the central SOE leaders. In the words of former SASAC Chairman Li, the biggest SOEs were to be cherished as "the eldest sons of the republic."

This "eldest sons" aristocracy currently has 117 members. That number decreases from time to time as the Party combines them in arranged marriages to strengthen their financial and industrial bloodlines. These "eldest sons" are bestowed monopoly and oligopoly positions in the Chinese economy. The leading luminaries in financial terms are China Petroleum & Chemical Corp., or Sinopec, ($273 billion in 2011 revenue), State Grid Corp. of China ($226 billion), Industrial and Commercial Bank of China ($80 billion), China Mobile Group ($76 billion), and China Railway Group ($69 billion).

There is no doubt that China's first decade of WTO membership and the simultaneous return to favoring SOEs under the Hu-Wen administration have been very lucrative for the SOEs. The privileges enjoyed by these entities were explained in the June 2011 study by Unirule, which is headed by reform-minded, eighty-three-year-old economist Mao Yushi. (Mao in May this year was awarded the Cato Institute's $250,000 Milton Friedman Liberty Prize.) Titled "The Nature, Performance and Reform of State-Owned Enterprise," the study shows that China's largest SOEs are indeed flush with profits, but that they lose money if their subsidies are subtracted.

Before digging into Unirule's results, it is important to understand the universe of SOEs included in the study. Unirule gave up trying to determine the exact number of SOEs in China. The report says, "according to some statistics" from 1998 to 2003, the number of state-owned and state-holding enterprises dropped to 150,000 from 238,000—and that by 2007 the total had fallen to an estimated 110,000.[43] The Unirule SOE profit and subsidy estimates are based on data from the NBS. The Unirule estimates endeavored to include all of the central SOEs as well as other large provincial and municipal SOEs that are prominent enough for the local SASAC organizations to track.

From 2001 to 2009, "reported profits of state-owned enterprises and state-holding industrial enterprises totaled RMB 5.8 trillion," the study said, going on to suggest that 2009 profits were nearly four times higher than in 2001. These profits are far from evenly distributed. For example, in 2010 the 125 central SOEs at the time accounted for two-thirds of the profits of all companies labeled as SOEs throughout China. In addition, 61 percent of central SOE profits, which totaled RMB 852.27 billion, came from just 10 of the big central SOEs in 2010.[44]

Reinforcing this finding is the degree to which profits are generated by the biggest SOEs with the tightest monopolies. For example, in 2006, nine SOEs accounted for 69 percent of the central SOEs' aggregate profit: PetroChina Company, Ltd., Sinopec, China National Offshore Oil Corp.

(CNOOC), China Mobile, China Telecom, Shanghai Baosteel Group Corp. (Baosteel), Aluminum Corp. of China (Chalco), China Shenhua Energy Co., and State Grid.[45] The total profits of China Mobile and Sinopec alone in 2009 surpassed the combined profits of China's 500 largest private enterprises.[46]

The Ten Most Profitable SOEs in 2010 (with profits)

- China National Petroleum Corp.: RMB 124.18 billion
- China Mobile: RMB 97.27 billion
- China National Offshore Oil Corp: RMB 74.23 billion
- China Petroleum & Chemical Corp.: RMB 72.12 billion
- Shenhua Group: RMB 46.86 billion
- State Grid Corp. of China: RMB 32.44 billion
- FAW Group Corp.: RMB 24.9 billion
- Shanghai Baosteel Group Corp.: RMB 19.88 billion
- China State Construction Engineering Group: RMB 14.38 billion
- China Ocean Shipping Group Co.: RMB 14.05 billion

The Unirule report also makes the case that, despite their overflowing coffers, China's SOEs have been returning almost none of their earnings to the government. "The recorded performance of SOEs is not a reflection of their real performance, but the result of numerous preferential policies and an unfair business environment," Unirule stated. "This unfairness is a result of fiscal subsidies from the central government, different financing costs, as well as subsidized land and resource rents.

These subsidies are important to track as China's national champion SOEs go global. When joining the WTO in 2001, China agreed to cancel all subsidies within the scope of the WTO's "Agreements on Subsidies and Countervailing Measures." While China did terminate certain supports, many of the original subsidies were continued in practice but submerged sufficiently deep in the bureaucracy to evade the scrutiny of those looking for evidence of trade violations. Unirule's economists mined the nooks and crannies of government budgets, bank lending records, and state economic plans to produce detailed estimates of SOE subsidies. These statistics don't include state-owned financial institutions. They also don't include the tens of thousands of smaller SOEs scattered around China that are showered with government funds and favors.

Key SOE Subsidies

By not paying the government for industrial land they occupy, from 2001 to 2009 the SOEs received a subsidy of RMB 3.9 trillion—which accounted for two-thirds of their total nominal profits.

SOEs paid an average real interest rate of 1.6 percent on their loans from the state banks from 2001 to 2008, as compared to a market interest rate average of 4.68 percent. This is equivalent to a subsidy of RMB 2.3 trillion in the form of foregone interest payments.

The SOEs from 2001 to 2009 underpaid taxes for oil, coal, natural gas, and other resources by RMB 497.7 billion.

Pocketed Profits

If the total RMB 7.5 trillion in subsidies and foregone costs uncovered by Unirule is deducted from SOE profits from 2001 to 2009, the real average return on equity for the SOEs in those years is *negative* 6.29 percent.

SOEs did not return any of their profits to the government between 1994 and 2007.

After 2007, only a trickle of SOE profits went to the government. A mere 6 percent of SOE profits were turned over to the state in 2009. This figure fell to 2.2 percent in 2010.

Taming Not Trust-Busting

Are SOEs exempt from China's Anti-Monopoly Law (AML)? Yes and No.

Since the AML went into effect in August 2008, the SOEs have been exempt from anti-monopoly regulators scrutinizing their monopoly or oligopoly positions. While the mergers and acquisitions (M&As) activities of foreign and Chinese private companies undergo extensive AML reviews, the SOEs have had a free pass on M&As as the government mandates mergers of SOE competitors within and across targeted sectors to develop economies of scale and cultivate SOE national champions.

But the AML is starting to be used as a tool for taming bad SOE behavior. This trend began in November 2011 when the NDRC revealed an AML investigation of China Telecom and China Unicom for using their dominance in broadband access to suppress competition.

The question going forward is whether the AML will truly be used as a trust-busting tool to promote real competition among state and non-state actors—or whether the AML will be employed by the Party to manage periodic outbursts of frustration from Chinese consumers.

This will be difficult to sort out due to the muddled mandates of SASAC, powerful sector-specific regulators such as the Ministry of Industry and Information Technology and the Ministry of Railways, and the AML enforcement authorities, an inherently weak, non-independent hybrid agency that includes the NDRC, the State Administration for Industry & Commerce, and the Ministry of Commerce.

When SASAC was formed in 2003, the agency was directed to "enhance the state-owned economy's controlling power" and encourage "state-owned capital to concentrate in major industries and key fields relating to national security and national economic lifelines" and "accelerate the formation of a batch of predominant enterprises with independent intellectual property rights, famous brands, and strong international competitiveness."

(continued on next page)

Five years later, Article VII of the AML said the "state protects the lawful business activities of business operators in sectors that affect the national economic lifeline and state security and are controlled by the state-owned part of the economy." It went on to say that state-owned companies must "operate in accordance with the law, act in good faith, implement strict self-regulation, accept monitoring by the public and may not use their controlling position or exclusive operation/exclusive sale position to harm the interests of consumers."

Former US Deputy Assistant Attorney General for Antitrust Jim O'Connell's recent article in *Antitrust* magazine expresses the legal community's confusion. "Is this language intended to set SOEs aside into a special category under the AML—where state oversight can be relied upon to protect consumer interests or where SOEs would simply be allowed to police their own conduct through self-regulation? Or is the language intended simply to recognize the unique nature of SOEs within the Chinese economy while also putting such companies on notice that the AML enforcement agencies—which are, after all, part of the 'state' that 'oversees and regulates the business acts and prices' of SOEs—will act to protect consumers from anticompetitive SOE conduct?" [47]

The allegations against China Telecom and China Unicom include charging competitors quadruple regular prices and cutting off access to customers who offered lower prices to competitors. Li Qing, deputy director of NDRC's (National Development and Reform Commission), Price Supervision & Anti-Monopoly Bureau, told reporters in November that the two SOEs face penalties of 1 percent to 10 percent of their annual revenues of more than $12 billion. The telecom giants reacted quickly. In December both companies asked for an end to the investigation and issued statements "admitting that their pricing practices were perhaps not what they should have been and pledging to cut broadband access rates and increase access speeds."[48] The NDRC hasn't reacted publicly, but the AML permits the agency to suspend and terminate investigations.

The State Advances, the Private Retreats

The resurgence of SOEs in recent years is immortalized in a four-character phrase: *guojin mintui*, which roughly translates as "while the state advances, the private retreats." The tale of two biotechnology companies in Shandong province suggests that even in the celebrated Strategic Emerging Industries sectors, SOEs can follow this practice of usurping private enterprise.

Cathay Industrial Biotech is a private biopharmaceutical company founded in 1997 that produces advanced ingredients for nylon by fermenting hydrocarbons in industrial vats. This ingredient, known as diacid, is used in a wide variety of products, ranging from lubricants to diabetes drugs. While other companies developed similar techniques using microbes to produce diacids, Cathay became an industry leader through a proprietary, cost-effective bio fermentation process. Cathay currently produces about half the world's industrial output of diacids.

The founder and CEO of Cathay, Liu Xiucai, could be a poster child for China's technology development dreams. Born in 1957 in a poor farm village, Liu studied chemistry in China and then headed to the US, obtaining a chemistry PhD in 1989 from the University of Wisconsin. After postdoctoral studies at Yale and Columbia universities, Liu worked on drug development at Sandoz Pharmaceuticals. He returned to China in 1994 to reverse-engineer and then produce drugs that had gone off patent in the US and Europe. With his earnings from that business, Liu created Cathay as a homegrown biotechnology firm, which quickly attracted tax breaks and other government incentives.

As Cathay refined its diacid fermentation process, the company became a major supplier to DuPont Co., and collected a $120 million investment from Goldman Sachs. The company was charging toward a successful stock market listing until 2010 when a competitor, Shandong Hilead Biotechnology Co. Ltd., began producing the same product 400 miles away—and slashing prices. Instead of listing, Cathay filed a lawsuit.

Cathay's attorneys told the *New York Times* that Hilead's technology was stolen by one of Cathay's deputy plant managers, Wang Zhizhou. Cathay's lawsuit asserts that Wang and six co-workers who left Cathay in 2008 stole the technology and founded Hilead along with Chen Yuantong, a scientist who had retired from the Chinese Academy of Sciences, and Cao Wubo, a wealthy entrepreneur with links to the Shandong provincial government.

The party secretary of Shandong put Hilead on the fast track, and the city of Laiyang offered government bank financing and arranged to house the company in its industrial park. A provincial infrastructure fund also earmarked more than $150 million for the company. The China Development Bank followed by pledging a $300 million loan. Propelled by its low prices, Hilead captured more than 10 percent of the global market within a year of opening. Chen Yuantong, now Hilead's chief scientist, in an interview with the *New York Times,* denied the accusations of trade secret theft.

Cathay has thus far been blocked from gathering evidence, according to the *Times* report. After filing the lawsuit last year, Liu worked his connections in Jining, the city where Cathay is located, to initiate a police investigation in order to gather evidence. Dispatched by the court, Jining police showed up at Hilead's factory gate in September 2011 only to be barred from entering because, officers were informed, Beijing had bestowed "national security" status on the complex.

Liu told the *New York Times* he "will not give up on this dream" even if he has to leave China to do so. "I'm Chinese, you know, so the Chinese government should want me to contribute. We're pioneers. If the Chinese government does not allow me to do this, I will find another place."[49]

Liu and his company apparently fell victim to a local power play, which was enabled by policies that are supposed to create home-growth technology pioneers like Liu. Despite the best intentions of some senior Party officials, China's technology innovation policies are instead pouring money into SOEs and leading to little scientific innovation, as we detail in Chapter Two.

Flying Against the Wind

The behavior of central SOEs often conflicts with the country's objectives. Back in 2006, Hu and Wen were pushing to strengthen SOE monopolies. Tsinghua University sociology professor Sun Liping warned that "monopolies and powerful industrial groups such as telecommunications, oil, electric power and automobiles recently have started to become special interest groups and have all begun to exert an obvious impact on the formulation of public policy."[50]

A clear example of this hit the headlines in 2007 after the State Council and SASAC approved China Eastern Airlines plan to sell 24 percent of its shares to Singapore Airlines. Feeling threatened by a hookup between a competitor and one of the world's best airlines, SOE national champion Air China scuttled the deal. The first step was for Air China to accumulate sufficient China Eastern shares to try to block shareholder approval of the deal. To do so, however, Air China needed to steamroll SASAC and the State Council. The regulators backed off after Air China chief Li Jiaxing was suddenly promoted head of the Civil Aviation Administration of China (CAAC), the country's aviation regulator. "We were naïve," said China Eastern CEO Li Fenghua. "We thought approval by the authorities would resolve all our difficulties."[51]

CHAPTER TWO

INDUSTRIAL POLICIES AND DECEPTIVE PRACTICES

China hopes for a great leap forward to global technology leadership through proactive industrial policies that support and subsidize SOEs and government research institutes. These policies are aimed at reducing reliance on foreign technology and maintaining the Party's control over China's industrial apparatus. They are fostering distrust in the diplomatic world, deception in business circles, and despoiling the scientific community at home.

Indigenous Innovation Sparks International Indignation

When President Hu and Premier Wen came into office in 2003 the state of Chinese science and technology was bleak, if not a bit embarrassing. Despite the expenditure of billions of RMB through thousands of government programs and projects, China was still struggling to innovate and invent. SOE managers were distracted by politics and perks, and China's best scientists rarely returned home after pursuing advanced degrees overseas.

So Hu and Wen placed "scientific development" at the top of their agenda, and Wen used his position as head of the Party's Leading Group on Science, Technology, and Education to coordinate an old-fashioned Soviet-style "big push" campaign. Some two thousand scientists, bureaucrats, and business managers were organized into twenty working groups to hammer out objectives and detailed plans. The result was a centrally planned, government-funded system focusing on sixteen megaprojects.

The landmark document that launched the campaign was named "The National Medium- and Long-Term Plan for the Development of Science and Technology (2006–2020)." Its authors described the plan as the "grand blueprint of science and technology development" to bring about the "great renaissance of the Chinese nation." Its stated goal was to transform the Chinese economy into a technology powerhouse by 2020 and a global leader in technology by 2050.

The plan explicitly stated that a key tool for creating China's own intellectual property (IP) and proprietary product lines would be through "enhancing original innovation through co-innovation and re-innovation based on the assimilation of imported technologies." But the complexity of the plan—in fact, less a plan and more a set of ever-changing laws, policies and regulations—meant few foreigners understood its implications.

The Sixteen Megaprojects

- Core electronic components, high-end general use chips, and basic software products
- Large-scale integrated circuit manufacturing equipment and techniques
- New generation broadband wireless mobile communication networks
- Advanced numeric-controlled machinery and basic manufacturing technology
- Large-scale oil and gas exploration
- Large advanced nuclear reactors
- Water pollution control and treatment
- Breeding new varieties of genetically modified organisms
- Pharmaceutical innovation and development
- Control and treatment of AIDS, hepatitis, and other major diseases
- Large aircraft
- High-definition earth observation system
- Manned spaceflight and lunar probe programs
- Three undisclosed projects believed to be classified and military in nature.

These became clear as most of the RMB 4 trillion in global financial crisis stimulus spending was pumped into the SOEs. These enterprises began to vigorously follow their instructions to absorb and assimilate foreign technology in their joint venture deals. International companies concluded that the Indigenous Innovation campaign constituted a blueprint for massive technology theft. Even a few prominent multinational CEOs who normally would complain only behind closed doors spoke out publicly. One of the most notable was General Electric CEO Jeff Immelt, who was quoted as saying, "I really worry about China. I am not sure that in the end they want any of us to win, or any of us to be successful."[52]

The Chinese government responded to the ensuing outcry with concessions—or at least the veneer of concessions. President Hu announced during a US state visit in November 2010 that China would moderate some of the more contentious policies. In July 2011, state media reported the government had scrapped three 2007 regulations that linked government procurement to Indigenous Innovation domestic content requirements.[53] It wasn't until November that the State Council released formal notice to nullify documents linking innovation policies to government procurement incentives.[54]

The jury is still out as to how seriously the government will implement this change. With these announced concessions, China maintains that the Indigenous Innovation issue has been completely resolved. However, many foreign businesses and governments are unconvinced. The procurement policies are just a fragment of the Indigenous Innovation–inspired impediments to foreign access to Chinese markets.

Making Up for Missed Opportunities

Party leaders went back to the drawing board in 2009. China wanted to avoid protracted battles with the United States, European Union, and many other governments that were searching for appropriate punitive trade actions. But the Indigenous Innovation policies were proving to be less than optimal for China as the stimulus money was funding as much SOE real estate speculation as it was basic research and scientific breakthroughs.

In concert with Vice Premier Li Keqiang, his likely successor, Premier Wen in 2009 organized a series of meetings and seminars involving the National Development and Reform Commission (NDRC), MIIT, the Ministry of Science and Technology (MOST), the Ministry of Finance (MOF), and other key agencies, as well as leading scientists and academics.[55] After sifting through China's numerous lists of "megaprojects," "strategic industries," "pillar industries," and "emerging industries," the group decided to combine these concepts under the banner of Strategic Emerging Industries. The goal was to select industries that were both vital to China's national economy and sufficiently cutting edge that global leaders in most cases had yet to emerge. Instead of playing catch-up with the West, the SEI initiative is aimed at China taking the lead in next-generation industries.

Wen spelled out his vision for the SEIs on the sixtieth anniversary of the Chinese Academy of Sciences in November 2009. "The scientific selection of the Strategic Emerging Industries is vital," he said. "If we choose correctly, we can leap forward with development. If we choose wrongly, we will have missed our opportunity." Wen stressed that China had to be successful this time as the country had missed four opportunities for technological modernization due to feudal thinking, international isolation, foreign oppression. and domestic political instability since the West began passing up China with the Age of Enlightenment and Industrial Revolution more than three hundred years ago.

President Hu reiterated Wen's call to action in a Politburo group study session on the SEIs in May 2011. Saying "we must seize this opportunity," Hu championed the SEI framework as "a necessary requirement for taking the initiative in international competition." Government ministries and commissions were directed to submit their own lists of Strategic Emerging Industries. After much debate, the State Council compiled a short list of nine. This was eventually narrowed to seven industries with thirty-seven sub-industries. The seven SEIs are ranked in order of importance. Clean Energy Technology is ranked first because of risks to the Party's political survival posed by the severity of the country's environmental problems. Second is Next-Generation Information Technology, which is considered a key to overall modernization, a process known as *lianghua ronghe*, or "using 'informatization' (a word coined by China) to spur industrialization."

The Seven Strategic Emerging Industries and Thirty-seven Subindustries

Clean Energy Technology: High-efficiency and energy saving, advanced environmental protection, recycling usage, reusing waste products.

Next-Generation IT: High-generation mobile communications, next-generation core Internet equipment, smart devices, internet of things, Three Network Convergence, cloud computing, new displays, integrated circuits, high-end software, high-end servers, digitization of culture and creative industries.

Biotechnology: Biopharmaceuticals, innovative pharmaceuticals, biomedicine, bio-agriculture, bio-manufacturing, marine biology.

High-End Equipment Manufacturing: Aerospace and space industries, rail and transportation, ocean engineering, smart assembly.

Alternative Energy: Nuclear power, solar power, wind power, biomass power, smart grids.

New Materials: New function materials, advanced structural materials, high performance composites, generic base materials.

Clean Energy Vehicles: Electric-hybrid cars, pure electric cars, fuel cell cars.

The SEI initiative has so far been short on details and long on confusing revisions. Announced funding plans have been all over the map. They have ranged from RMB 4 trillion in October 2010 to RMB 14 trillion in March 2011. In November 2011, Vice Premier Wang Qishan "confirmed" RMB 11 trillion in talks with US officials.[56] Party media outlets the next day reported that this was only a "rough estimate."

The NDRC, MOF, and MOST met in October 2011 to discuss the overlapping relationship between the SEIs and Indigenous Innovation megaprojects. The group decided that the megaprojects would serve as an "engine" to drive implementation of the SEIs. The government is gradually releasing detailed development plans for each SEI and its related subindustries. Responsibility is split between NDRC and MIIT. NDRC is handling Clean Energy Technology, Biotechnology and Alternative Energy. MIIT is taking charge of High-End Equipment Manufacturing, New Materials, Next-Generation IT, and New Energy Vehicles.[57]

Voluntary Is the New Mandatory

Perhaps the biggest lesson learned from the kerfuffle over Indigenous Innovation forced technology transfer policies was to no longer spell out the most controversial requirements in black and white. Verbal instructions and requests to "volunteer" one's technology are today's rules of the road.

The best example of voluntary regulations is a policy known as Management Methods for Controlling Pollution by Electronic Information Products Sold in China. The international acronym for this type of policy is RoHS, or Restriction of Hazardous Substances. China's RoHS is a version of similar frameworks developed in the European Union, United States, and other countries. But that strategy and the method of implementation of China's RoHS demonstrates how China learned a lesson from the fallout over the blatantly strong-armed Indigenous Innovation policies. The simple addition of the word "voluntary" has eliminated any tool foreign companies might have had at their disposal to mount a resistance.

This refined form of RoHS policy has been five years in the making. The first phase of RoHS came in 2007 with labeling requirements for consumer electronics products. Companies were simply required to list the quantity of any of six restricted materials: lead, mercury, cadmium, hexavalent chromium, PBB, or PBDE. In comparison to the EU's RoHS standard, which has served as the global model, China's RoHS covered more products and placed the burden of compliance on more actors. Nonetheless, foreign companies found the policy to be manageable.

That changed when the second phase rolled out in October 2011. This is when "voluntary" made its debut. The enhanced RoHS regime bans products that contain hazardous substances above certain thresholds. It also enacted a National Recommended Voluntary Certification program managed by MIIT and the Certification and Accreditation Administration of China (CNCA). This procedure allows companies to "voluntarily" submit products listed in a catalog to state laboratories for extensive testing in order to obtain RoHS certification. In addition to the wasted time, extra costs, and extensive paperwork involved, foreign companies and governments are concerned that these state laboratories may provide Chinese competitors access to their intellectual property.

Once certified, products are expected to qualify for incentives that include tax breaks and government procurement preferences. Being shut out of procurement is no small matter. If SOEs and local government procurement are added to central government purchasing, China's government procurement market accounts for more than 20 percent of GDP.[58] The first edition of the catalog includes three product categories—cell phones, landline phones, and printers—and a more extensive list is expected soon.

China RoHS is considered by foreign trade officials and technology company attorneys as an archetypal example of how China has learned to employ the word "voluntary." By making the certification scheme optional, China has armed itself with a rejoinder to accusations that it has created yet another business barrier. Companies and trade organizations that have pushed back are told they are welcome to sit on the sidelines. But given the hyper-competitive Chinese market, companies that don't "volunteer" will be essentially shut out of the market.

The benefits of employing the "voluntary" adjective don't stop there. Under the WTO's Technical Barriers to Trade rules, voluntary environmental labeling policies are much less regulated than mandatory ones. Since participation is optional, China was required only to *notify* the WTO rather than submit the RoHS policy to review. This creative packaging of RoHS also demonstrates China's increased sophistication in anticipating and heading off criticism from foreign entities. In past policy disputes, China often failed to liaise with or inform relevant international organizations. With RoHS, China notified WTO of the coming changes and solicited comments from foreign companies. Uncharacteristically, MIIT even participated in discussions with the international business community regarding RoHS. None of this brought about substantial policy changes. Complaints about RoHS being a cleverly packaged trade barrier are now met with rebuttals that China is simply protecting the environment and responsibly regulating hazardous substances.

Clean Energy Technology: Cryptic Standards

China has begun producing increasingly high-quality industrial and technology standards that are attracting international interest and acceptance.

China's early attempts to produce homegrown standards—such as its WAPI standard for wireless local area networking, and its TD-SCDMA standard for third-generation cellular communications—were widely seen as technical failures. These efforts were part of a national campaign to create Chinese technological and industrial standards, as China felt exploited by paying royalties to foreign IP rights holders.

The power of China's domestic market and state-led economic system is employed to establish Chinese standards at home before taking them global. ZUC—encryption algorithms named after a famous Chinese mathematician—provides a blueprint of how this is done.[59]

ZUC is China's encryption algorithm for its 4G LTE mobile telecom standard.[60] It was approved by the European Telecommunications Standards Institute in September 2011. This internationalism is not a sign of increased openness. It is instead an excuse to force foreign companies to use China's own LTE standard in the Chinese market and to use the scale of the market to encourage its adoption abroad. This has been accomplished through the voluntary-is-mandatory method. Without explicitly mandating the ZUC standard, China announced in November 2011 that only domestic encryption algorithms could be used for 4G in China. Not long after that, MIIT and the State Encryption Management Bureau called a meeting of industry players and told them that in practice ZUC implementation would be mandatory.

The incentive to adopt ZUC globally is very strong, as China is the world's largest cell phone market. Diplomats and industry analysts say that plans are underway to follow this same pattern with standards under development for smart grid and cloud computing.

Driven to Distraction

Chinese planners expected all-electric vehicles to become the poster child of success for the Strategic Emerging Industries initiative. [61]

No country is as well positioned as China to lead the global transformation to electric cars and trucks. The country has the largest automobile market in the world, with at least another eight hundred million people yet to reach the middle class. SEI funding would drive technology development and manufacturing. The Party could order nationwide construction of charging stations and other necessary infrastructure as well incentivize SOE carmakers to build electric cars ahead of consumer demand. And the debilitating air pollution in Chinese cities and the country's reliance on imported oil provides powerful motivation. That was the theory, at least.

But the SEI initiative for New Energy Vehicles (NEVs) has sputtered. One reason is technology overreach. Another is that the restriction limiting foreign automakers to fifty-fifty joint ventures with Chinese SOEs has begun to backfire. The joint ventures operated by Volkswagen, General Motors, Toyota, Nissan, Hyundai, Honda, and the other global auto powers dominate the China market. While their SOE partners are rolling in cash, private Chinese automakers struggle for market share due to difficulties in obtaining financing and an inability to keep pace with the latest technology. The NEV initiative was envisioned as a way for Chinese companies to take the lead in electric vehicles. MIIT's initial NEV plan designated certain Chinese majority-owned ventures to develop core electric car technologies. The big three: batteries, motors, and control systems.

It didn't take long for these electric vehicle ambitions to crash into technological and bureaucratic walls. Chinese auto companies did not have the technology to produce workable or commercially viable electric vehicles. This helped fuel ferocious bureaucratic infighting over the NEV policy. MOST was the chief proponent of pure electric vehicles. A few SOE national champions angled for control of the NEV infrastructure. State Grid, for example, saw the development of NEV charging stations as within its protected territory. But CNOOC and Sinopec, sensing a threat to their gas and diesel earnings, also sought to capture the opportunity. A former government official and auto expert said that the NEV policy's technology overreach turned it into "a big scam" that involved "the government lying to industry and industry lying to the media—and all of them lying to each other."[62]

More pragmatic figures in the NDRC and MIIT sought a compromise focusing on hybrid models. Premier Wen intervened by writing an article for the Party magazine *Qiu Shi* that warned against committing resources to premature technologies. This triggered a strategic retreat. But China retains its ambitions for global leadership on NEVs. The central government's updated *Foreign Investment Catalog*, published in December 2011, moved nearly all technologies associated with NEVs into the "encouraged" category. This suggests that China wants to first focus on foreign companies building the technology supply chain in China that can support Chinese leadership on electric vehicles somewhere down the road.

Innovation 2.0 Meets Bureaucracy 101

The Three Network Convergence (*sanwang ronghe*) SEI initiative to unify media delivery technologies has been a three-ring circus.

The opening act came in 2001, well before the SEI initiative, when the State Council announced that telecom, broadcast, and the Internet would be merged into a single platform.[63]

The plan invaded the territory of very powerful and obstreperous bureaucracies. MIIT backed Internet Protocol TV (IPTV) to deliver television over the Internet as that would fall under its jurisdiction.[64] The ministry fought hard for telecom operators to be allowed to offer their own IPTV platforms. The State Administration of Radio, Film, and Television (SARFT) focused on maintaining its regulatory grip by promoting digital television delivery through cable or terrestrial TV signals—and defended its turf by regularly blocking licenses for IPTV.[65]

(continued on next page)

The State Council announced in January 2010 that Three Network Convergence would be a top SEI priority. Four months later, SARFT and MIIT announced a compromise involving shared jurisdiction. Broadcast companies would manage content. Telecom operators would handle transmission. They basically agreed to use IPTV technology under the management of SARFT.[66] Efforts to integrate the municipal networks began.

But two years later, IPTV had a paltry fourteen million subscribers as infighting between MIIT and SARFT continued.[67] SARFT may have control on paper, but MIIT has continued to push for supervisory rights and for a bigger share of the profits.[68] This past January, forty-two cities were chosen for trial networks. But arguments over standards, and who controls those standards, continue to impede progress. Local broadcasters and the large telecom SOEs are responding by boycotting the process and moving ahead with a mishmash of deals to offer digital TV through telecom and cable networks and bypass the official convergence efforts.

Cloudbursts of Cash

With cloud computing considered the next big thing for the Internet, China's initiative for cloud computing was also envisioned to be an early SEI success. Funding is flowing, and enormous cloud computing centers are under construction across China. But this SEI initiative appears to be as focused on real estate speculation as it is science or technology services.

Cloud computing powers some of the world's most popular Web-based services, including elements of Amazon, Facebook, Google, Evernote, and many e-mail services. It promises a cyber-world in which users can access, sync, and share their personal data at the touch of a button from any device connected to the Internet.

Becoming a cloud computing powerhouse is a logical goal for a country with more than half a billion Internet users. For this initiative, a subset of Next-Generation IT, the government plans to invest $173 billion,[69] of which $154 billion will go to fixed-asset investment in the five pilot cities of Beijing, Shanghai, Guangzhou, Wuxi, and Hangzhou.[70] Government money is also flowing into Chinese companies. Alibaba Group (China's e-Commerce trading platform) and Baidu, Inc. (China's home-grown Google) have together received more than $240 million.[71] The big telecom SOEs are also investing heavily in cloud computing.

Lofty Plans for the Cloud

- Beijing's "Cloud of Blessing": three square kilometers, $8 billion investment, fifty thousand employees.
- Shanghai's "Asia-Pacific Cloud Computing Center": $3 billion investment.
- Langfang (unnamed hub): 580,000 square meters, aims to be the largest in the world.
- Chongqing's "Liangjiang International Cloud Computing Center": three-kilometer-long data center, $6 billon investment over five years, claims it will allow foreign companies to bypass the Great Firewall entirely.
- Others: Guangzhou's "Cloud of Sky," Wuxi's "Cloud Valley," and Hangzhou's "Cloud Supermarket."

The government is encouraging international leaders in cloud computing technology to establish joint ventures with Chinese companies. Such companies as Microsoft Inc., Dell Inc., and IBM Corp. are seizing the opportunity. Though the government is still formulating the relevant legislation, foreign companies are expected to be limited to a 50 percent stake in any joint ventures, in keeping with China's limits on Value-added Telecom Services (VATS). The providers may also need an Internet Content Provider (ICP) license. To apply for the VATS and ICP licenses, the companies must form a special joint venture known as a Foreign Invested Telecommunications Enterprise (FITE). Obtaining approval for a FITE is very difficult. These complications will put foreign cloud services providers at risk of losing their intellectual property to Chinese companies that have ICP licenses.

The Business Software Alliance, a US trade association, in June published a report entitled "Lockout" that details China's cloud services and other discriminatory technology policies. The report warns that "IT protectionism" restrictions that are modeled on Chinese policies are spreading to Brazil, India, and other countries "masked as policies to promote innovation, enhance security, or advance other domestic priorities." BSA President and CEO Robert Holleyman said: "This makes them far more difficult to challenge using traditional WTO rules or trade remedies. We need a new trade agenda for the digital economy."[72]

As the foreigners fret, local governments in China are bubbling with ambitious plans for cloud centers. In addition to the five pilot cities, a couple dozen other cities have indicated plans to build cloud hubs. Chinese officials, scientists, and tech executives are already complaining that real estate speculation is too often the real priority. A Beijing city official said in an interview that many local governments are donning "cloud computing hats" to reap real estate profits.[73] Professor Li Deyi, a member of the Chinese Academy of Engineering, recently warned, "The development of cloud computing cannot be turned into a game of land and capital possession."[74] And Rui Xianglin, senior vice president of German software giant SAP AG, has said that the infrastructure is springing up too quickly, wasting money and taking the focus off the services each cloud center will actually provide.[75]

Some Chinese government officials admit that a big obstacle to China becoming a cloud computing leader is the country's reputation as a center of industrial cyber-espionage and trade secret theft. Cloud computing demands total trust. Information and data stored on cloud computing center servers has to be protected and kept private. Foreign multinationals so far display almost no interest in storing their information in the Chinese cloud. Technology research firm International Data Corp. says that even big Chinese companies are reluctant to do so. "The propensity to outsource in China is the lowest in the region," the firm's research director told the *New York Times,* because big companies want to "keep control of IT assets."

In 2010, only 4 percent of companies were using cloud-based services in China. This compares to 16 percent in tiny Singapore. The companies gravitating to cloud services in China at this point are mostly smaller enterprises looking for ways to cut costs.[76]

Mutually Assured Deception

China's mercantilist technology and industrial policies and the global economic downturn have combined to create a damned-if-you-do, damned-if-you-don't dilemma for many foreign businesses in China.

Leading technology and industrial companies can't afford to stay away from China, as it is the world's principal growth market. As "China 2030," the report jointly published by the DRC and the World Bank, puts it: "Perhaps the most important global megatrend is the rise of China itself. No other country is poised to have as much impact on the global economy over the next two decades. Even if China's growth rate slows as projected, it would still replace the United States as the world's largest economy by 2030," and China's "share in world trade could be twice as high" as the US share.[77]

It's no wonder, then, that the CEOs of many multinationals believe that failure to succeed in China could result in the eventual downfall of their companies on a global scale. But these CEOs are also aware that access to the China market often requires handing over their technology to a Chinese SOE partner—one that could be expected to go global and compete against the same foreign company that provided the technology. "For many of us, the China market is a matter of survival," said a former China CEO of a leading industrial multinational. "So when it comes to implementation, the foreign companies find ways to protect themselves by taking advantage of confusing terms and conditions in the contracts and doing whatever we can to not transfer the complete technology."[78]

This CEO and others describe a process that begins with mutual distrust between Chinese and foreigners at the outset of contract negotiations. It is common for the Chinese RFP (request for proposal) to require detailed technology specifications and demand that 100 percent of the technology be handed over by the end of the contract. The foreign bidders try to protect themselves by littering their proposals and final contracts with wiggle-room wording and conflicting language to circumvent the most serious technology-transfer requirements. Once the actual business cooperation begins, this distrust quickly shifts to a game of mutually assured deception. When it's time to transfer their know-how to the joint venture, the foreign companies often "black-box" their most valuable technology. This is done by withholding technical design details and packaging their components or systems in ways that are difficult to dissect and reverse-engineer.

The result may be as dangerous as these partnerships are disingenuous.

During a lightning storm in July 2011, two high-speed trains collided near the city of Wenzhou in Zhejiang Province. Forty people were killed and at least 192 injured. In a fifty-page report published in December following public outrage over the crash, the State Council blamed the crash on a signaling system that was supposed to prevent train collisions. The report concluded that poor system design in combination with lightning strikes was responsible.

Outside of official government circles, however, the black-boxing of technology is believed to have been a contributing factor to the crash.

The signaling system was assembled by Beijing-based Hollysys Automation Technologies Ltd., a Nasdaq-listed company that was once part of the Ministry of Electronics. Hollysys, one of the three companies China's Ministry of Railways (MOR) had approved to do such work, received more than $100 million in high-speed rail signaling contracts in 2010, according to a *Wall Street Journal* investigation. "An examination of China's use of foreign technology in its bullet-train signal systems highlights deep international distrust over China's industrial model," the *Journal* said. The Hollysys signaling technology contained circuitry tailor-made by Hitachi Ltd. of Japan. Worried about losing its technology, Hitachi provided black-boxed components with the inner workings concealed from Hollysys. A senior Hitachi executive told the *Journal* that Chinese engineers probably couldn't fully comprehend the technology as Hitachi withheld the technical blueprints. "It's still generally a mystery how a company like Hollysys could integrate our equipment into a broader safety-signaling system without intimate knowledge of our know-how," the Hitachi executive told the *Journal* in October last year.[79]

Hitachi had good reason to be wary. Foreign companies are forbidden from bidding on China's high-speed rail contracts. Their only option is to partner with Chinese SOEs that plan to become their global competitors. But the help these foreign companies offer to China is rewarded with shrinking market share. Industry figures show that foreign companies account for 15 to 20 percent of China's investment in the rail sector, with their earnings roughly the same as eight years ago.[80]

Black-boxing to protect proprietary technology could have implications beyond high-speed rail. To realize its nuclear power ambitions, not to mention its desire to build its own commercial airliner, the C919, China needs to depend on foreign technology. The only way for foreign companies to participate in these sectors, however, is through joint ventures and technology sharing with a Chinese partner.

In the nuclear sector, China is adopting technologies from France, Canada, Russia, and the United States. This has scientists worried about China's ability to master and continually improve all of these complex technologies. "It is extremely dangerous—in terms of standardization of design, operational safety, and ease of maintenance—for any nation to run so many different types of reactor simultaneously," a Carnegie Endowment for International Peace researcher wrote. "China's leaders should immediately limit further diversification of nuclear reactors and concentrate the nuclear sector's human and financial resources on the research, development and commercialization of just one or two types of standardized design."[81]

Unsafe at Any Speed

The State Council said corruption also likely contributed to the July 2011 train crash. It occurred a half year after the arrest of Railways Minister Liu Zhijun, known as "Great Leap Liu" for seeking to build the world's fastest trains in the shortest time possible. Chinese media reports claimed Liu had eighteen mistresses and had skimmed tens of millions of dollars from rail projects.

(continued on next page)

Caixin Media's *Century Weekly Magazine* reported that 80 percent of all high-speed rail projects were awarded to two SOE contractors: China Railway Group and China Railway Construction Corp. Executives at two suppliers of high-speed rail equipment said that until 2011, MOR used an "expert review" system for choosing contractors in which middlemen paved the way for contracts.

MOR accrued colossal debt during Liu's eight-year tenure as minister. By the end of 2010, according to *Century Weekly*, MOR had accrued RMB 1.25 trillion (almost $200 billion) in outstanding loans. Industry analysts estimate that debt payment plus interest were set to hit RMB 250 billion in 2011, while MOR cash flow from operations would not exceed RMB 200 billion.[82] The Beijing-Shanghai high-speed railway was initially estimated at $1.96 billion. In the end, it cost $3.4 billion. Cost of the Guangzhou South Station escalated to RMB 14.8 billion from an initial estimate of a couple billion RMB. "This is because every project is contracted, subcontracted and subcontracted again," a contractor told the magazine. "If you want to profit from the plan, you have to continuously modify the plan."[83]

In March this year, a three-hundred-yard section of high speed rail track collapsed on a line under construction in central China—after having passed inspection and test runs. The *People's Daily* reported that the contractor had cut costs by packing dirt instead of gravel under the tracks. A Fujian Province rail contractor told the *New York Times* that bribes to government officials erase profits unless savings can be found. "You are constantly being forced to cut corners, or else you cannot make a profit," the contractor said. "Everyone does this."[84]

Please Leave Home Without It

The forced technology transfer features of Chinese industrial policies have generated deep distrust. But industrial cyber-espionage and cyber-hacking from China is prompting companies to act as if business in China constitutes a form of economic warfare.

In an October 2011 report to Congress, fourteen US intelligence agencies identified China as the No. 1 threat to US firms through cyber-hacking and the theft of trade secrets.[85] While the report detailed many Chinese government policies that appear to support and encourage these activities, the intelligence agencies stopped short of saying the Chinese government is directly involved. Some analysts believe that SOE national champions—under tremendous pressure to innovate but incapable of doing so—are significant drivers of Chinese industrial cyber-espionage.[86] "Chinese actors are the world's most active and persistent perpetrators of economic espionage," the US government report stated. "US private sector firms and cybersecurity specialists have reported an onslaught of computer network intrusions that have originated in China, but the IC (intelligence community) cannot confirm who was responsible."[87]

According to the October 2011 report to the US Congress, the areas most threatened are:

- Information and communications technology, which forms the backbone of nearly every other technology.
- Business information that pertains to supplies of scarce natural resources or that provides foreign actors an edge in negotiations with US businesses or the US government.
- Military technologies, particularly marine systems, unmanned aerial vehicles and other aerospace/aeronautic technologies.
- Civilian and dual-use technologies in sectors likely to experience fast growth, such as clean energy and health care/pharmaceuticals.

It should be no surprise that seriously schizophrenic behavior by multi-nationals in China is becoming the norm. CEOs continue to display big smiles and voice "win-win" rhetoric when visiting. But their in-country executives often behave as if they are working behind enemy lines. Corporate conference calls discussing anything remotely sensitive no longer take place on Chinese telecom networks. Some multinationals don't even trust the Hong Kong phone system. They instead require executives to travel to South Korea to make important calls, or fly home for face-to-face meetings. Many technology multinationals and foreign governments forbid their people from bringing smart phones or laptops to China, and some US government officials are forbidden to connect to the government network (.gov) from within China's borders.

Ken Lieberthal, a former top Clinton administration China policy-maker who now heads a China center at the Brookings Institution, described his own protocol to the *New York Times*. Instead of his own electronics, he brings a "loaner" cellphone and laptop, and he wipes the laptop clean upon his return. In China, his phone never leaves his sight and during meetings he turns it off and removes its battery to avoid having the microphone turned on remotely. To bypass any key-logging software, he brings his Internet passwords on a flash drive to copy and paste them rather than typing them in.

As Jacob Olcott, a cybersecurity expert at Good Harbor Consulting, told the *Times*, "Everybody knows that if you are doing business in China, in the 21st century, you don't bring anything with you. That's 'Business 101'—at least it should be."[88]

Based on available information regarding attacks from China, Russia, and other countries, a former FBI agent estimates that the total value of the information stolen from corporate networks in 2011 reached almost $500 billion.[89] Respected analysts, including James Mulvenon, a cybersecurity expert at Defense Group Inc., believe there is ample evidence to show that China is responsible for the vast majority of this loss. Google Inc., DuPont, Johnson & Johnson, and General Electric represent just a few of the companies that have admitted losing proprietary data to hacker-thieves, and several (including Google) have publicly pointed to China as the source of the intrusions.[90]

In December last year Bloomberg obtained intelligence data indicating "at least 760 companies, research universities, Internet service providers and government agencies were hit over the last decade by the same elite group of China-based cyber spies." Bloomberg said that the companies "range from some of the largest corporations to niche innovators in sectors like aerospace, semiconductors, pharmaceuticals and biotechnology."[91]

"What has been happening over the course of the last five years is that China—let's call it for what it is—has been hacking its way into every corporation it can find listed in Dun & Bradstreet," Richard Clarke, former special adviser on cybersecurity to President George W. Bush, told an October 2011 conference on network security. "Every corporation in the US, every corporation in Asia, and every corporation in Germany—and using a vacuum cleaner to suck data out in terabytes and petabytes. I don't think you can overstate the damage to this country that has already been done."[92]

The Chinese government steadfastly denies these accusations. Given the ability of hackers to mask their location and affiliations, it has been impossible to gather court-ready evidence implicating Chinese authorities in cyber-theft. Six of the seven cases adjudicated in the US in 2010 under the Economic Espionage Act involved Chinese nationals. Some of these cases were limited to corporate espionage aimed at business gains. But others clearly involve economic espionage in which the state is both the guiding hand and the final beneficiary of the criminal activity.[93]

The DuPont Case

In February this year, Walter and Christina Liew were charged with stealing trade secrets from DuPont and selling them to several state-affiliated Chinese companies. The trade secret in question is DuPont's titanium-oxide technology, a fifty-year old process with applications in military and aerospace paints.[94] Walter Liew is accused of earning $20 million from a series of sales that took place between 1998 and 2009.[95]

(continued on next page)

According to a *Wall Street Journal* investigation, along with the Liews, five Chinese SOEs were named as defendants. This represents the first time the Justice Department has pursued espionage charges against a foreign SOE.

Prosecutors claim direct involvement by the Chinese government. In a 2004 letter to the Pangang Group, a state-owned conglomerate based in Sichuan, Walter Liew claimed that a high-ranking Party member asked him in the early 1990s to bring titanium technology to China. Liew now says he misrepresented that he had direct senior Party contacts. But one of his co-defendants recently declared under oath that he himself was goaded into the theft after Chinese government officials "overtly appealed to my Chinese ethnicity and asked me to work for the good of the PRC." A spokesperson for the Chinese Embassy in Washington denied any government involvement, claiming, "Chinese businessmen behave on their own behalf." [96]

The Sinovel Wind Group Case

Sinovel Wind Group Co. is China's largest wind turbine maker. It was also once the biggest customer of American Superconductor Corp. (now AMSC), accounting for more than 70 percent of annual revenue.[97] In June 2011, AMSC discovered that Sinovel had paid a now-incarcerated employee of WindTec, an AMSC subsidiary, $1.5 million to hand over proprietary wind turbine technology.[98] Five months later, AMSC filed four lawsuits worth $1.2 billion in China against Sinovel for theft of trade secrets and for failing to honor existing contracts.[99]

(continued on next page)

Though Sinovel is publicly listed on the Shanghai Stock Exchange, the company's ties to the state are clear. Its founder and president is Han Junliang, a former senior executive of state-run Dalian Heavy Industries, a major Sinovel shareholder. According to a Bloomberg investigation, Han has a close relationship with Zhang Guobao, who until recently headed China's National Energy Administration which is responsible for wind energy industry project approvals. One of Sinovel's main shareholders is New Horizon Capital, a company co-founded by Winston Wen, the son of Premier Wen Jiabao.[100]

Since the technology theft last year, AMSC has lain off more than one-third of its employees, and the company's market capitalization has collapsed. After filing the lawsuits against Sinovel, AMSC was hit by a crippling cyber-attack that is now under investigation by the FBI.[101] Meanwhile, Sinovel has replaced GE as the world's second-largest wind turbine maker, behind Vestas of Denmark.

The four AMSC complaints—and two Sinovel countersuits—are still working their way through Chinese courts. One of the suits has been appealed to China's Supreme Court after being dismissed by a provincial court. The evidence against Sinovel led Senate Foreign Relations Committee Chairman John Kerry to call the case a "red-hot, smoking gun example" of technology theft by China.[102]

CHAPTER THREE

THE CONUNDRUM OF AUTHORITARIAN CAPITALISM

Peeling back the layers of China's economic onion reveals a world of weak oversight, obsessive secrecy, murky accounting, and unrestrained power. At the core of the system, behind a façade of market listings, audit firms, and government regulators sits the Chinese Communist Party, the chief architect and beneficiary of China's authoritarian capitalist system.

The Tip of the Iceberg

Looking only at the stock market listing of Chinese SOEs provides a very superficial view of the Chinese business world.

Of the more than five hundred Chinese companies currently listed on overseas stock markets, about two hundred are SOEs.[103] Among them are some of the national champion SOEs that have become the international face of China Inc. To analyze China's state sector by focusing on the slivers of SOEs that are chipped off and polished up for listing is akin to inspecting an iceberg and ignoring everything below the water line. Nonetheless, the world's investment banks, stock analysts, multinational bosses, politicians and many business journalists persist in viewing China's state sector by fixating on the tip of the SOE icebergs, not the murky mass that lies below.

Of the sixty-nine companies[104] from mainland China in the Fortune Global 500 in 2012, only seven were not SOEs: Shagang Group, Ping An Insurance (Group) Co. of China, Ltd., China Pacific Insurance Group, Shandong Weiqiao Pioneering Group, Zhajian Geely Holding Group, China Merchants Bank, and Huawei Technologies Co. Ltd. All of these companies have received significant government assistance and most count government entities among their shareholders.

China opened the door for select SOEs to list on overseas stock markets in 1993. Then-Premier Li Peng and other conservative leaders were convinced to take this step by a group of young reformers who had returned from US universities. Their mentor was current Vice Premier Wang Qishan, who at the time was a vice governor of China Construction Bank. Wang convinced Li and other Party leaders that listing Chinese SOEs on foreign exchanges was a smart way to get money from foreigners without giving up control of the companies. Wang and his group of reformers were always careful to avoid using the word "privatization" when discussing the market listings with Party leaders.[105]

Ka-ching!

In 1997, China banked its first $1 billion-plus initial public offering (IPO) with China Mobile's dual-listing in Hong Kong and New York.

In August 2000, Sinopec's $3.5 billion listing represented the first simultaneous Chinese stock listing in New York, London, and Hong Kong.

In October 2005, China Construction Bank's $8 billion Hong Kong listing was the world's largest IPO since 2000.

In June 2006, Bank of China set a new record with an $11.2 billion Hong Kong listing, and then raised another $2.5 billion in Shanghai a month later.

In October 2006, Bank of China's four-month old record was shattered by Industrial and Commercial Bank of China's $21.9 billion dual-listing in Hong Kong and Shanghai—the world's largest-ever IPO at the time.

In September 2007, Construction Bank went public again—this time in Shanghai—raising $7.6 billion.

By early 2010, Chinese SOEs had raised $262 billion on international exchanges.[114] And this does not include the July 2010 public offering of the Agricultural Bank of China, the world's largest-ever first-time share sale, valued at $22.1 billion.

The listings sent an avalanche of cash into SOE bank accounts. Shareholders, however, have been mostly frozen out of influencing how the SOE groups and parent companies operate. Proper monitoring would assume that the listed portion of these SOEs are market-driven, have independent decision-making power, and are accountable to their boards of directors and shareholders. However, their real role is to carry out Party policies while making money from their monopolies, subsidies, and privileges. As Columbia University Law School professors Li-Wen Lin and Curtis J. Milhaupt put it in their November 2011 study of China's state sector: "The government attempts to ensure that company-level behavior results in country-level maximization of economic, social and political benefits."[106] In short, the Chinese government is the only shareholder that really matters.

Prior to listing on foreign exchanges, Chinese companies on occasion have been somewhat forthcoming about this. In its 2003 New York Stock Exchange (NYSE) disclosure China Telecom stated, "We will continue to be controlled by China Telecom Group, which could cause us to take actions that might conflict with the best interests of our other shareholders." Chalco said something similar in its 2002 disclosure: "The interests of our controlling shareholder, who exerts significant influence over us, may conflict with ours."[107]

There is also a common misperception that a significant portion of these SOE shares are publicly traded. In reality, the state controls the majority—usually the vast majority—of the shares. This is the case with all the Chinese SOE behemoths on the Fortune 500. Only 30 percent of China Mobile is publicly listed. Less than 20 percent of Sinopec's 86.7 billion shares traded on the overseas exchanges,[108] while more than 75 percent are owned by the controlling shareholder, Sinopec Group.[109]

Sprawling and Soaring

China's national champion SOEs often control dozens, if not hundreds, of subsidiaries. This reflects their origins as government ministries. The Aviation Industry Corp. of China (AVIC) is a prime example.

According to AVIC's website, the group includes twenty-two listed companies, nearly two hundred subsidiaries and more than four hundred thousand employees. AVIC reported $71.2 billion in assets and $31 billion in 2010 revenue. A banner on its website says AVIC strives to reach RMB 1 trillion in sales (about $150 billion) by 2020. AVIC's current configuration came from a 2008 merger between China's civilian and military aviation groups in accordance with Hu Jintao's policy of "civil-military integration" (*junmin jiehe*).[110] AVIC now

(continued on next page)

spans across defense, transport aircraft, aviation engines, helicopters, avionics, general aviation aircraft, aviation research and development, flight tests, trade and logistics, and asset management. AVIC says on its company website that "to strengthen the military and to enrich the people" is its core mission.

That core mission involves a web of partnerships between the world's aviation leaders and the Commercial Aircraft Corp. of China (Comac). AVIC is the controlling shareholder in Comac. Other Comac shareholders include such SOE national champions as Chalco, Baosteel Group, Sinochem Group, and Shanghai Guosheng Corp., Ltd. Comac is leading AVIC's quest to build a Chinese rival to Boeing and Airbus.

The current focus is on a competitor to the Boeing 737 and Airbus 320 called the C919. By mid-2011, Comac had signed more than thirty Sino-foreign JVs to obtain aviation technology.[111] For the C919, Honeywell supplies power units, on-board computing systems, wheels and brakes; Rockwell Collins handles the navigation system; GE Aviation is building the avionics; Eaton Corp. is handling fuel and hydraulics; and Parker Aerospace is responsible for flight controls. Powering the aircraft will be engines built by CFM International, a JV between GE and French conglomerate Safran.[112] Though the C919 is still under development, some 235 planes have already been ordered. The customers are mostly from domestic SOE national champion airlines.[113]

State Secrets and Inaudible Auditors

SOEs and private Chinese companies listed in the US are increasingly citing state secrets and refusing to provide required audit information to US regulators.

Today's trend of withholding information and citing state secrets is possible because the definition and scope of China's state secrets laws are broad, vague and, well, secretive. In March 2010, SASAC issued the "Regulation on Protection of Trade Secrets by Centrally Administered State-Owned Enterprise," which established that a wide range of commercial information can be considered state secrets.[115] The law is broad enough that any information about the 117 central SOEs could be defined a state secret. This has also encouraged Chinese private and state-private hybrid companies to jump onto the state secrets bandwagon—especially when they find themselves under investigation.

China High Precision Automation Group Ltd. is a Hong Kong–listed manufacturer of a variety of technology products, ranging from quartz watch movements to industrial automation equipment, including instruments used by China's Shenzhou spacecraft.[116] In October 2011, the company's stock was suspended from trading after its auditor KPMG declined to sign off on its books.[117] After the Fujian Province–headquartered company said it couldn't provide information that KPMG considered important for its audit—because some of its products were "related to aerospace and other fields which are classified as state secrets"—KPMG resigned as auditor.[118]

Deloitte's Chinese affiliate finds itself in a similar bind with a private Chinese company that sells mostly to SOEs. In May 2011, Deloitte resigned as auditor for NYSE-listed Longtop Financial Technologies after it was unable to confirm Longtop's cash balances at local banks. A provider of financial software to such heavyweight SOEs as the major banks, insurance companies, State Grid, CNOOC, and China National Tobacco, Longtop's stock was suspended from trading that same month.[119] An investigation by the US Securities and Exchange Commission (SEC) and the Public Company Accounting Oversight Board (PCAOB) is currently under way. When the SEC and PCAOB requested Longtop audit documents, Deloitte refused, saying, "Turning over [its Chinese affiliate's] work papers could violate Chinese law prohibiting the disclosure of 'state secrets.'" Deloitte's US spokesperson said Deloitte was "caught in the middle of conflicting demands by two government regulators."[120]

US and Chinese regulators are now in a standoff over the right to assess these auditors. As of December 2011, there were 143 Chinese companies listed in the US with audits unavailable to the PCAOB, an industry oversight body established by Sarbanes-Oxley in 2002 in response to Enron and other US accounting scandals.[121] The PCAOB is legally required to inspect all auditors of companies listed in the US. But China, citing state sovereignty, has so far rejected US requests to assess the Chinese auditors. "We can't simply pretend that China is different," said James Doty, PCAOB chairman. "You can't come sell your securities here and ignore the fact that the law requires and people want to know that the auditor's been inspected."[122]

This dispute is taking place just as China's Ministry of Finance seeks to create national champion audit firms. The auditors of the overseas listed Chinese companies are usually China affiliates of the Big Four audit firms—KPMG, Deloitte, Ernst & Young, and PricewaterhouseCoopers. Barred from establishing independent entities in China, the foreign firms set up twenty-year joint ventures in the 1990s, and those are now reaching expiration. The MOF is focused on reducing the role of foreign auditors by developing ten large domestic accounting firms—with a goal of at least three of them ranking among the world's top twenty firms.[123] To accomplish this, MOF is pressuring the expiring joint ventures to transform into limited partnerships owned by Chinese CPAs (certified public accountants).[124] In May, the MOF announced that by 2017 no more than 20 percent of the partners in the Big Four firms in China can be foreigners—and the senior partners must be Chinese citizens.[125]

In July, Bloomberg reported that China Development Bank had earmarked just over $1 billion in loans to help Chinese companies delist from US stock markets. The state-owned policy lender, which is charged with financially supporting China's economy and companies, aims to help the Chinese companies move to exchanges in Hong Kong and China.[126]

The Iron Rice Bowl Becomes a Pot of Gold

China's state banks are cash machines for the SOEs.

On a national level, the state banks supply the money for creating national champion SOEs and carrying out the underpinning industrial policies. On a local level, even money-losing SOEs are granted state bank credit to preserve jobs and generate tax revenue for local governments.[127] Though sporadic reforms have tried to push them toward commercial lending practices, the state banks are a "basic utility" to provide capital for "cherished state-owned enterprises," said Carl Walter and Fraser Howie in their book *Red Capitalism*. Simply put, "the banks are the financial system."[128]

The Truly Colossal Big Four Banks (even by Chinese standards)

Industrial and Commercial Bank of China has $2.04 trillion in assets and 397,339 employees.

China Construction Bank has $1.64 trillion in assets and 313,867 employees.

The Agricultural Bank of China has $1.569 trillion in assets and 444,447 employees.

The Bank of China has $1.587 trillion in assets and 279,301 employees.

China's SOE-dominated banking system also may be the most stubborn impediment to comprehensive economic reform.

China has the highest level of state ownership of banks of any major economy. SOE banks are the dominant source of capital and the underwriters of nearly all risk. The Big Four—Bank of China, China Construction Bank, Industrial and Commercial Bank of China (ICBC), and Agricultural Bank of China—together control 43 percent of China's total financial assets. (In comparison, foreign banks together hold less than 2 percent of Chinese assets.)[129]

The government shareholder for the Big Four banks is Central Huijin Investment Ltd., a wholly owned subsidiary of the state sovereign wealth fund China Investment Corporation. As with the non-financial SOEs, the Party appoints the top brass, many of whom also hold Party leadership positions. ICBC Chairman Jiang Jianqing, for example, serves on the Seventeenth Party Central Committee. Vice Premier Wang Qishan and China central bank Governor Zhou Xiaochuan both are past SOE bank bosses.[130] These ties directly into the Party hierarchy help the banks carry out their main duty of "patriotic banking," as *The Economist* recently termed it. Their paramount role is to serve the Party's agenda, despite many attempts over the years to make them more commercially oriented.

In purely financial terms, China's leading banks serve the least efficient companies. According to several studies, including McKinsey's "Putting China's Capital to Work: The Value of the Financial System," productivity in China increases with each form of ownership that moves progressively away from direct state-ownership.[131] This is consistent with the OECD's conclusion that private companies are twice as productive as wholly state-owned enterprises.[132] As the McKinsey report puts it, China's state banking sector has "fallen short in its task of allocating credit to the most productive players in the economy." Consequently, SOE banks lack the risk assessment skills and procedures needed to manage true commercial banks.[133]

For the past decade bank reform has been sidelined as Party leaders focused on refueling the SOEs and financing industrial policies. After the global economic downturn cranked open the government's policy lending spigots in 2008, $1.4 trillion in loans gushed into SOEs, local governments, and infrastructure projects. At least 30 percent of these loans, dubbed by the Chinese press as the "Great Leap Forward of Lending," are believed to be in default.[134]

The Fragile Fortress

In *Red Capitalism*, Carl Walter and Fraser Howie describe China's banks as a "fragile fortress" with few defenses in the battle against bad loans from policy-directed lending. Unrestrained lending in the late 1980s and early 1990s created a mountain of non-performing loans (NPLs). Between 1999 and 2008 alone, an estimated $480 billion in bad loans were transferred to newly created asset management companies (AMCs). Bank of America, Goldman Sachs, and other blue chip banks then invested in the Big Four SOE banks, giving them a coating of credibility for incredibly successful IPOs.

The AMCs purchased the bad loans at full face value because discounting these loans could have bankrupted the SOE borrowers. The government bonds involved in those transactions came due in 2009. Repayment would have required the AMCs to write off an estimated RMB 1.5 trillion in losses. But this would have bankrupted the AMCs and brought chaos to the financial system. The State Council punted by approving a ten-year extension on the bond repayment deadline. Analysts suggest that when the 2019 deadline arrives, Chinese policymakers may have no choice but to kick the can another decade down the road. [139]

Despite their chronically imprudent lending habits, SOE banks are kept afloat—and reap huge profits to boot—through government-set interest rates. With a ceiling on the interest rates for deposits and a floor on lending rates, China's banks have enjoyed a comfortable spread of about three percentage points, which guarantees profits. Economists describe the result as "financial repression," since depositors' savings are eroded by inflation and private companies go starving for capital. "The financial system serves the interests of the national champions quite well, even if it serves private firms very poorly," the Columbia Law School study stated. [135]

The DRC–World Bank "China 2030" study expressed concerns that this SOE credit addiction could seriously hinder banking reforms. Pointing out that the average debt/equity ratio of SOEs exceeds 230 percent, the authors said, "If the financial system is liberalized, many highly leveraged SOEs would face difficulties in financing their investment or debt at low cost, deteriorating their financial situation and possibly leading to insolvency."[136]

Nonetheless, in early April Premier Wen suggested that breaking the monopoly of the Big Four banks is necessary to get sufficient financing to the entrepreneurs and smaller enterprises that China depends on for jobs and economic growth. "Frankly, our banks make profits far too easily," Wen said at a roundtable discussion. "Why? Because a small number of major banks occupy a monopoly position, meaning one can only go to them for loans and capital. That's why now, as we are dealing with the issue of getting private capital into the finance sector, that means we have to break up their monopoly." The Party's leading news outlets, the *People's Daily* and *Xinhua*, did not report his remarks.[137]

Nonetheless, in April this year China began announcing modest financial sector openings. The yuan has been allowed to float in a wider daily trading range. Banks have been given a bit of flexibility in setting lending and deposit rates. Foreign investors have been given increased access to China's stock and bond markets. Openings for Chinese private investors in the banking sector are also under discussion. Analysts say that this may be motivated by the need of state banks to gather capital to cover the nonperforming loans created during the global financial crisis lending binge.

The initiatives steer Chinese private investors toward investing in rural banks. But they can't be the main shareholder. The main sponsor threshold for these banks has been reduced to 15 percent from 20 percent. But the main sponsor must be a financial institution. "Only several dozen banks can be sponsors for rural banks, and they don't have the incentive to have a private company on board," Zeng Gang, the research chief at CASS's Institute of Finance and Banking told *Caixin Online*. "Lowering the stock requirement gives more options to the sponsor bank, not private capital."[138]

The Largest and Most Idiosyncratic Shareholder in the World

SASAC may be both the world's largest shareholder and the world's weakest shareholder. Nonetheless, as a recent study put it, "Even beyond this disjuncture in its formal status and powers, SASAC is unique as the focal point for state capitalism in a rapidly rising economic superpower."[140]

The commission was created in 2003 to be the controlling shareholder in China's SOEs after the enterprises were extracted from their parent government entities and converted into a variety of corporate structures and industry groupings. But SASAC has since struggled to accumulate real clout. As a government organization, it is trumped by the Party.

The Party's Central Organization Department maintains a tight grip on its power to appoint the top SOE bosses. A typical SOE leadership team includes the party secretary, several deputy party secretaries, and a secretary of the Discipline Inspection Commission, the anti-corruption organization. At the same time, the original parent government ministries and regulatory masters of the SOEs also maintain blurry but strong lines of authority over central and local SOEs.[141]

The 2008 Law of the PRC on State-Owned Assets of Enterprises, enacted after fifteen years of contentious debate, was supposed to demarcate the parameters of SASAC's authority as controlling shareholder. Instead, SASAC's administrators were left bracketed by ambiguity. The law designates SASAC as the controlling shareholder of SOEs, accompanied by the rights of an investor. But the law doesn't provide comprehensive definitions of those rights, nor does it delineate enforcement mechanisms. Instead, it disperses authority. "The State Council and the local people's governments may, when necessary, authorize other departments or bodies to perform the investor's functions for state-invested enterprises on behalf of the corresponding people's government," the law states.[142] While ambiguous about SASAC's role, the statute very clearly outlines the duty of SOEs to "safeguard the basic economic system of China . . . giving full play to the leading role of the state-owned economy in the national economy."

If SASAC's positioning with the SOEs isn't vague enough, the commission has only nominal authority over local SASACs in the provinces and municipalities. The local SASACs are appointed by and report to their local governments—not to central SASAC. A recent study for the US Congress estimated that there are some 30 provincial-level and 270 municipal-level SASACs.[143] A SASAC spokesman in Beijing said that his organization didn't know how many local SASACs there are in China.[144]

The local SASACs in different regions also have distinctive governance scopes—a situation the central government has been trying of late to address. The initial focus has been on getting some control of local SOE financial institutions. Starting in 2009, the State Council began standardizing local SASAC operations and nudging local SOEs into their orbit. Central SASAC Vice Minister Huang Shuhe said in August 2011 that twenty-eight provincial SASACs and seventy municipal SASACs now had oversight of their local state-owned financial assets. He also said that the local SASACs in China's provincial level cities—Beijing, Tianjin, Shanghai, and Chongqing—had gained oversight of the SOEs in their jurisdictions. Central SASAC's goal is to better integrate with local SASACs during the Twelfth Five-Year Plan. [145]

Central SASAC is by far the most important when it comes to global trade and international business. That is because of its responsibility for the 117 central SOEs that form the main pool of national champions. SASAC is under a Party mandate to encourage the SOEs to become more efficient, profitable, and accountable—and to go global. "The national champions represent much more than a purely financial investment for the party-state," the 2011 Columbia Law School study said. "SASAC, as the organizational manifestation of the party-state in its role as controlling shareholder, seeks to maximize a range of benefits extending from state revenues to technological prowess, and from soft power abroad to regime survival at home."

On paper, SASAC appoints some SOE executives to their posts, supervises their compensation, approves any increase or reduction of company capital, reviews outbound investment plans, and certifies changes in corporate structures. Prior to the formation of SASAC, SOE bosses decided on their own pay packages. Today, SOE managers receive base pay, bonuses, and long-term incentive compensation. The average 2009 pay of the CEOs at the central SOEs under SASAC was about $88,000, with about two-thirds of that performance-based, according to a 2010 speech by Li Rongrong, SASAC chairman at the time.

In reality, this can be just a fraction of their total compensation, as SOE executives receive a buffet of such benefits as cars and drivers, housing, medical care, education, and side payments for various services to the company. The 2011 Columbia Law School study suggests that even the executive pay approved by the boards and disclosed to directors of the SOEs listed on stock markets "is something of a fiction." Some companies have disclosed that their executives "donate" this money back to their parent companies.[146] Ultimately, their real compensation is often undisclosed—and unknown to SASAC.

SASAC continues to face an uphill struggle to establish real authority. The chairman of SASAC is a ministerial-level position. This means that the SASAC chairman receives the same salary and perks as China's cabinet ministers. But the SASAC chairman does not sit on the State Council as cabinet ministers do. Fifty-three of the top SOE bosses that the SASAC chairman is supposed to supervise carry the same ministerial rank as he does. Leaders of the largest SOEs, such as the CEOs of the three national oil companies, outrank the SASAC chairman.[147]

Even the annual personnel exchange system—in which fifty to sixty SOE managers are seconded to SASAC, and a similar number of SASAC staff are sent to SOEs for one-year stints—shows where real power lies. SASAC largely seconds to the SOEs junior employees who have no real monitoring or oversight authority. The SOE representatives sent to SASAC, however, are generally senior staff who can exercise significant influence over SASAC policies affecting the SOEs.[148]

Given SASAC's muddled mandate and weak legal power, it has evolved into both a supervisor of and a supplicant to the central SOEs. SASAC is gaining some influence over international investments by the SOEs through a $10 billion fund aimed at strengthening the SOE national champions through overseas acquisitions of technologies and companies. Nonetheless, since SASAC shares oversight with so many others, and lacks real power over top executive appointments and other key aspects of SOE management, "SASAC is not only the largest controlling shareholder in the world, it is also quite possibly the most idiosyncratic," said the authors of the Columbia Law School study.[149]

In the Shadow of the Party

In official literature, the Central Organization Department is described as the Party's human resources arm. But that doesn't even start to describe the extent to which the department's influence permeates the state sector and much of the private sector as well.

Because the department manages the appointments of all senior Party officials, its director is one of the Party's most important and formidable figures. The current director, Li Yuanchao, is considered a frontrunner to become a member of the Party's top decision-making body, the nine-member Central Standing Committee.

Since the Party reaches into just about all aspects of life in China—including politics, economics, business, society, education, media, entertainment, culture, recreation, police and courts, the military, and diplomacy—the Organization Department is essentially the world's most powerful headhunter, human resource manager, and behind-the-scenes personnel puppet master. In *The Party*, Richard McGregor paints a vivid portrait of the Organization Department by describing what a comparable entity in the United States would look like:

> A similar department in the US would oversee the appointment of the entire US Cabinet, state governors and their deputies, the mayors of the major cities, the heads of all federal regulatory agencies, the chief executives of GE, ExxonMobil, Wal-Mart, and about fifty of the remaining largest US companies, the justices of the Supreme Court, the editors of the *New York Times* and the *Washington Post*, the bosses of the TV networks and cable stations, the presidents of Yale, Harvard, and other big universities, and the heads of think tanks like the Brookings Institution and the Heritage Foundation.[150]

Princely (and Princessly) Positions

Party officials consider SOEs a fitting place for their children to carry out the Party's agenda, learn business skills and, in many cases, gather assets for the family.

Hu Haifeng (b. 1971), son of President Hu Jintao, former president of Nuctech, a Tsinghua University-owned company that has been a monopoly supplier of security equipment to Chinese airports, is party secretary of Tsinghua Holding Co. Ltd.

Wen Yunsong, son of Premier Wen Jiabao, is chairman of China Satellite Communications Corp. (China Satcom), the country's monopoly satellite operator.

Li Xiaopeng (b. 1959), son of former Premier Li Peng, was president of China Huaneng Group and Huaneng Power International before he was appointed vice governor of Shanxi Province in 2010.

Li Xiaolin (b. 1961), daughter of Premier Li Peng, is CEO of Hong Kong–listed China Power International Development.

Zhu Yunlai (b. 1957), son of former Premier Zhu Rongji, is CEO of China International Capital Corp., one of China's largest investment banks.

Li Huidi (b. 1969), son of Li Changchun, one of the top nine Party leaders in China as a member of the Politburo Standing Committee, is deputy general manager of the China Mobile Group.

Tan Zuojun (b. 1968), grandson of Tan Jiashu, former vice commander of the Air Force, is general manager of China State Shipbuilding Corp.

Kong Dong (b. 1950), son of Kong Yuan, the first commissioner of PRC Customs, is general manager of China National Aviation Holding Co.

Chen Hongsheng (b. 1950), son of Chen Zhengren, former party secretary of Jiangxi Province, is chairman of the China Poly Group Corp.

Ren Kelei (b. 1950), son of Ren Zhongyi, former party secretary of Guangdong, is general manager of Overseas Chinese Towns Enterprises.

The Organization Department appoints the three top executives of the 53 most important of the 117 central SOEs that are under SASACs purview. In most cases, this includes the party secretary, chairman of the board, and the CEO. The CEO in many SOEs simultaneously has the role of party secretary. Most of these positions carry a ministerial or vice-ministerial rank in the Party.

The top deputy posts in these enterprises are appointed by SASAC, but not by the personnel division of SASAC. Instead, the Party Organization Department *within* SASAC, known as the Party Building Bureau, chooses these people. Executive appointments for the other SOEs are appointed by bureaucrats in SASAC's "Second Bureau," in collaboration with the relevant supervising ministries and Party organs. The appointments must be approved by the State Council.[151]

With the Organization Department as the Party's human resources hub, the SOE bosses and government leaders are players in extraordinary games of musical chairs between government and various SOE posts. The behemoth telecom and oil SOEs are classic examples. In 2004, due to concerns that the telecom bosses were becoming too powerful, the Party reshuffled the top executives of the three biggest publicly listed telecom companies. Within hours of the announcement, the stock prices of all three dropped, with China Unicom losing 4.3 percent.[152] Party leaders in April 2011 ordered a similar reshuffle of China's three major national oil companies: Sinopec, CNOOC, and China National Petroleum Corp. (CNPC). Su Shulin, party secretary and general manager of Sinopec, was appointed to be deputy party secretary and acting governor of Fujian Province. He was replaced at Sinopec by Fu Chengyu, the party secretary and general manager of CNOOC. Wang Yilin, a senior executive at CNPC, was appointed as CNOOC's chairman and party secretary. "The oil executive reshuffle was a blatant reminder of the CCP's control over China's flagship firms," Erica Downs of Brookings and Michal Meidan of the Eurasia Group said in a recent monograph.[153]

The Party is increasingly inclined to move SOE bosses into top government posts. The reason is that the government officials often lack sufficient business experience to manage today's huge and complicated state companies. Since the SOE leaders tend to be younger, more highly educated, and have more extensive overseas experience, the Party believes that their inclusion in elite politics could make the Chinese government more global minded and business savvy.[154] According to Cheng Li of Brookings, these "state entrepreneurs" are gradually becoming "a new source of CCP leadership."[155] The Eighteenth Party Congress, in the fall of 2012, will likely witness the promotion of more SOE leaders to the Party's Central Committee.

SOE Leadership a Proven Path to Top Government Positions

Zhou Yongkang (b. 1942), a member of the powerful Politburo Standing Committee and head of the Central Political and Legislative Committee since 2007, which makes him China's internal security czar. He spent most of his career in the petroleum industry during the 1960s and 1970s. From 1985 to 1988 he was vice minister of the now defunct Ministry of Petroleum Industry. Zhou was general manager and party secretary of China National Petroleum Corp. from 1996 to 1998 before he became minister of Land and Resources in 1998 and 1999 and minister of Public Security from 2002 to 2007.

Wang Qishan (b. 1948), vice premier since 2008, alternated his career between People's Bank of China and China Construction Bank as vice president, president, and party secretary from 1989 to 1997. From 1998 to 2000 he was vice governor of Guangdong Province. From 2003 to 2007 he was deputy mayor and mayor of Beijing, and executive chairman of the Beijing Olympics Committee.

Jia Qinglin (b. 1940), chairman of the Chinese People's Political Consultative Congress since 2008, was general manager of China's National Machinery and Equipment Import and Export Corp. from 1978 to 1983. Jia was governor of Fujian Province from 1991 to 1993 and then party secretary until 1996. From 1997 to 2002 he served as deputy mayor, mayor and party secretary of Beijing.

(continued on next page)

Zhang Qingwei (b. 1961), governor and deputy party secretary of Hebei Province since 2012, was chairman of China Commercial Aircraft Company Ltd. from 2008 to 2012.

Zhu Yanfeng (b. 1961), vice governor of Jilin Province since 2007, was president of First Automobile Works Group Corp. (FAW) from 2000 to 2007. He held other positions at the FAW Group from 1983 to 2000.

Shang Fulin (b. 1951), chairman and party secretary of the China Banking Regulatory Commission since 2011. He was vice chairman of People's Bank of China from 1996 to 2000. He then became chairman of the Agricultural Bank of China. From 2002 to 2011 he was chairman of China Securities Regulatory Commission.

CHAPTER FOUR

A LOCAL REPERTOIRE
ON THE
GLOBAL STAGE

China's unique brand of authoritarian capitalism—along with the country's emergence as a global financial, economic, and trading power, and the practice of protecting domestic markets to enrich and empower national champion SOEs—has created a mismatched interface between China and the established global systems for governing trade and investment. Neither the WTO nor the array of bilateral dialogues and dispute resolution bodies has dealt with anything like this before. China's challenge threatens to push the existing systems to a breaking point. But China is also the biggest beneficiary of current configurations.

Out of Africa and into the World

China's "going out" initiative is pushing the corporate progeny of authoritarian capitalism into the world of global business. Their reception, and performance, is mixed.

China's national champion SOEs, working hand in hand with the Party, are the vanguard of China's global business ambitions. Commerce Minister Chen Deming made this clear during an August 2011 symposium when he heralded the national champion SOEs as "the backbone of China's going out strategy." [156] Several months earlier, SASAC vice chairman Huang Danhua said that "the construction of Party organizations overseas" would be the key to ensuring overseas success for Chinese companies.

Chinese overseas investment has been growing rapidly since 2005, when SOEs started striking significant deals for resource assets overseas. The Heritage Foundation estimates that between then and 2011, Chinese outbound investment has totaled $309 billion. The foundation also estimates that four companies—China National Petroleum Corp., Sinopec, China Investment Corp., and Chalco—account for roughly half of Chinese overseas investment since 2005. [157]

This all began quietly in 1996 when Jiang Zemin visited Africa. China's hyper-growth was stimulating an insatiable appetite for natural resources. China was seeking to diversify export markets and establish beachheads in the developing world, where Chinese companies could develop localized marketing, supply chain management, and customer service skills. Jiang saw Africa as the perfect place to start. The continent was blessed with abundant oil, minerals, and other natural resources. African consumer and industrial goods markets were a good match for the low-cost, no-frills products that sold so well in China. The Chinese leadership also felt that their SOEs would feel more comfortable working with Africa's dictatorships than the democracies of the developed world. [158]

An investment and resource-extraction bonanza followed. Ten years later, in November 2006, Chinese leaders welcomed forty-eight African leaders to Beijing for a two-day "Forum on China-Africa Cooperation" during which $2 billion in trade deals were accompanied by Chinese pledges to provide Africa with $3 billion in preferential loans and $2 billion in export credits. A $5 billion fund to encourage Chinese investment in

Africa was also announced. A month before the summit, the Chinese government cancelled its bilateral debt with thirty-one African countries. "Chinese assistance to Africa is sincere, unselfish, and has no strings attached," Premier Wen Jiabao told the gathering.[159]

China has made great contributions in Africa. Chinese funded infrastructure projects are visible all across the continent: roads and bridges in Congo, railways in Angola, power stations in Zambia, mass transit systems in Nigeria, a telecommunications network in Ethiopia, high-voltage power transmission lines to connect countries in Southern Africa, and a $600 million dam in Ghana.[160] Building these infrastructure projects also has provided Chinese SOEs with valuable experience in overseas construction. By the end of 2010, China had invested some $40 billion in more than two thousand enterprises in fifty African states.[161] China has also become Africa's biggest trading partner, with trade tripling in three years to reach $166 billion in 2011. China now buys more than a third of its oil from Africa, importing 1.5 million barrels per day from the continent in 2010.[162]

The interaction between China and Africa isn't always smooth. Zambia is a case in point. Chinese companies have invested about $2 billion and created some twenty thousand jobs in Zambia in recent years. But anti-Chinese sentiment is now widespread. In 2006, six African coal miners were shot during a wage protest at the Chinese Chambishi copper mine. Five years later, a group of one thousand miners at Chambishi were fired by the Chinese management after launching a wage protest.[163] In 2010, eleven African miners were shot by Chinese managers at the Chinese Collum Coal Mine in southern Zambia during labor protests. Two years later at the same facility, Zambian miners killed a Chinese supervisor during wage riots.[164] Michael Sata—complaining that "Zambia has become a province of China"—was elected president of Zambia last year on a strident anti-China platform.[165]

Chinese officials admit that even with some one million nationals living in Africa, their learning curve on the continent is steep. Zhong Jianhua, Chinese ambassador to South Africa from 2007 to 2011, is now the government's special envoy for African affairs. In an interview with Caixin's *Century Weekly* magazine in March this year, Zhong offered this explanation of the difference between how Western companies and Chinese companies operate on the continent. Instead of gathering an experienced staff, conducting feasibility, environmental, and technical studies, and liaising with the local government and community as multinationals would do, Zhong said, "A Chinese company usually brings a bag of money to the table. It would send three people, maybe two of whom can't speak English. . . . Some Chinese entrepreneurs think bribing a South African government official is enough."[166]

At the Forum on China-Africa Cooperation in Beijing in July 2012, President Hu pledged $20 billion in loans to African countries over the next three years. Hu said that the money would be aimed at helping Africans through such initiatives as a training program for thirty thousand Africans, providing eighteen thousand scholarships, and dispatching fifteen hundred medical professionals to Africa. He emphasized that African nations and China should cooperate to counter the influence of wealthy nations that seek to exploit Africa. "We should oppose the practices of the big bullying the small, the strong domineering over the weak and the rich oppressing the poor," Hu said at the forum.[167]

The prospect of bargains in the United States and Europe since the global financial crisis are drawing more Chinese companies to the developed world. Crisis-hit Europe has been the shopping area. China is scooping up European technologies and brands. In the auto sector, Chinese companies have acquired the MG Car Company Ltd., and AB Volvo, and entered into a strategic cooperation with the Daimler Motor Company.[168] Great Wall Motor has set up a car plant in Bulgaria. China's largest homegrown carmaker, Chery Automobile, is establishing a separate brand for Europe with production facilities in Italy.[169]

China has found it harder to gain traction in the United States, but investments are nevertheless ramping up. Political opposition to some early deals still spooks some Chinese investors. The most notorious case was CNOOC's $18.5 billion bid in 2005 for Unocal Corp., the largest attempted overseas acquisition by China at that time. The Chinese oil company withdrew its bid after Chevron Corp. offered a higher price and Congress voted 398–15 to call for reviewing the CNOOC deal as a threat to national security.[170] CNOOC has since come back with major investments in the United States. To avoid politics and learn how to operate in the United States, CNNOC has concentrated on co-investments with US energy companies. Most prominent are CNOOC's investments of more than $2.2 billion with Chesapeake Energy in shale oil and gas projects in Texas, Colorado, and Wyoming.[171] With the announcement in late July of CNOOC's proposed $18.2 billion acquisition of Canadian oil company Nexen, the US government is likely to be called upon by CNOOC to approve its acquisition of Nexen's assets in the United States, including in the Gulf of Mexico.

Chinese investments in the United States are increasingly diverse and ambitious. In January 2012, Sinopec reached a $2.42 billion deal with Devon Energy Corp. to help develop several shale fields in Ohio, Michigan, and elsewhere.[172] A month later, State Grid was reported to be in talks with US power firm AES Corp. about taking an 80 percent stake in its US wind power business. Analysts estimate the assets to be worth around $1.65 billion.[173] In May 2012, the US Federal Reserve approved the acquisition of an 80 percent stake in the American arm of Bank of East Asia by three Chinese financial institutions.[174]

China has reached into Hollywood with the Dalian Wanda Group Co.'s $2.6 billion purchase of AMC Entertainment in May this year. The deal makes the private Chinese company the world's largest theater operator.[175] The Shenzhen New World Group Co. bought the Sheraton Universal hotel for $90 million just months after paying $60 million for the Los Angeles Marriott Downtown.[176] As China increasingly focuses on strategic technologies, the government is encouraging Chinese companies to use international mergers and acquisitions to make up for the innovation gap at home. In upcoming years the purchase of technology companies in Europe and the US is expected to grow quickly. In 2009, China made the list of top ten global investors. The country is expected to invest $1 to $2 trillion abroad by 2020.[177]

The Reigning Champ
of All National Champions

While most of the large SOEs have yet to go beyond China's borders, China UnionPay has achieved the national champion trifecta: a rock-solid domestic card transaction monopoly, ownership of a proprietary "re-innovated" technology standard, and a global network poised to compete against the world's leaders.

This champ of all national champions was created in 2002 by People's Bank of China (PBOC), China's central bank, to handle the payment transactions of all credit, debit, pre-paid, and other payment cards in China. With this monopoly position in China's payment and clearance sector, UnionPay has relegated foreign credit card firms to operating in China through co-branded, dual-currency credit cards. The cardholders can purchase goods within China in RMB and overseas in foreign currencies. In China, the US banks and credit card companies handle the RMB transactions for co-branded cards through UnionPay. Outside of China, the co-branded card transactions are handled by the foreign banks. By leveraging its monopoly, UnionPay is rapidly expanding around the world. The company claims to have partnerships with some four hundred financial institutions in nearly one hundred countries—and that 2.3 billion UnionPay cards have been issued globally.

To accomplish this feat, China has had to openly violate a key WTO commitment. In its WTO Services Schedule, China committed to allowing foreign financial institutions to independently provide "all payment and money-transmission services, including credit, charge and debit cards" in foreign and local currency by December 11, 2006. That deadline passed with no action and the United States repeatedly attempted to negotiate a remedy in bilateral meetings between 2007 and 2009. US banks and credit card companies remained behind the scenes, worried that UnionPay would retaliate against the co-branded cards that give them a toehold in China.

MasterCard and Visa have the most co-branded, dual-currency cards in China. Due to a dispute with UnionPay over transaction processing, however, Visa is currently blocked from starting any new business in China. The dispute was triggered in 2009 when Visa warned UnionPay to stop processing international transactions for co-branded cards through the

UnionPay system. Previously, for the offshore US dollar transactions, UnionPay had been using Visa's system, as do all of Visa's partners. Union-Pay refused to comply. The dispute became public in June 2010 when Visa announced that it would block holders of dual-currency cards from using UnionPay's service when travelling overseas. At the time, UnionPay was already blocking Visa from expanding its co-branded card business in China.

Three months later—and nearly four years after China ignored the payment services compliance deadline—the USTR filed a WTO case. Though the September 2010 filing was based on four years of discussion among the USTR and Visa, MasterCard, American Express, and other major payment services providers, the US officials found little support beyond Visa for taking action, as the companies feared retaliation from China. And, sure enough, UnionPay soon announced deals with the competitors of leading agitator Visa. The very day of the WTO filing, Master-Card said it had signed an agreement with UnionPay aimed at "mutually beneficial business development."[178] Two months later, American Express signed an agreement with UnionPay to "explore the expansion of their current cooperative activities" and "establish working teams to develop potential new areas of cooperation."[179]

While the foreign credit card industry distanced itself from the WTO case as fast as it could, governments have embraced it. The United States was joined in the filing by the EU, Japan, Australia, India, South Korea, and Ecuador. Hearings before a WTO dispute resolution panel took place in October and December 2011.

A somewhat confusing decision was handed down in July 2012.[180] The panel ruled in favor of the United States but equivocated on the monopoly issue. The panel rejected US claims that UnionPay has an across-the-board monopoly for processing of all card transactions in China. The United States lost on this point because it failed to prove that China had declared a monopoly. The WTO accepted arguments that UnionPay's role in the market does not preclude the participation of foreign players, even though UnionPay has the only unified payment system in China and foreigners have been excluded from establishing their own systems.

Instead, the panel ruled that UnionPay violates WTO protocols through a monopoly on RMB transactions for payment cards issued in China. The panel also decided that China is in violation of WTO rules by requiring that all cards in China carry the China UnionPay logo, that all cards must be interoperable with the UnionPay system, and that Chinese merchants accepting card payments must post the UnionPay logo and use UnionPay's transaction system. "We are hopeful that this ruling will pave the way for international payment companies to participate in the domestic payments marketplace in China," Visa spokesman Will Valentine said after the ruling.[181] Both sides have sixty days to appeal the ruling.

Leading credit card companies are worried that once UnionPay has a large enough international footprint, the SOE will grab global market share through price cutting. "UnionPay is not really a commercial entity," said a foreign banker who has done business with the company since its inception. "If they want to lock in some market share they can really cut the price and get the business."[182]

UnionPay also hopes to use proprietary technology to capture global market share. In 2005, PBOC and UnionPay jointly developed the PBOC 2.0 Standard, a Chinese technical and security standard for "smart cards" that have chips instead of magnetic strips. The Chinese standard is based on, but not compatible with, the global EMV standard used by Europay, MasterCard, and Visa (hence the acronym EMV), as well as other major firms. China's goal is to have all cards in top-tier cities converted to the UnionPay smart cards by 2015.[183]

This initiative has created a great deal of uncertainty for foreign card companies since China could use it to phase out dual-currency cards. As it controls the transaction transmission for all point-of-sale and ATM terminals in China, UnionPay could, with the flick of a switch, eliminate the primary source of income in China for foreign players.

With its PBOC heritage and backing, UnionPay is a political powerhouse. It also serves as a retirement perch for many former PBOC officials. UnionPay Chairman Su Ning and his predecessor Liu Tinghua were both vice governors of PBOC. "UnionPay is a retirement stop to earn money for these officials," said the foreign banker. "UnionPay has the best of both worlds. They have the resources and the central bank's backing. Even the biggest banks can't challenge them."[184]

The WTO has been unable to meet the challenge of UnionPay because of a process that began more than a decade ago on the shores of the Persian Gulf.

Coming to Terms with China's Trade Juggernaut

Two events in Doha, Qatar, in November 2001 triggered profound and permanent changes in global trade: after sixteen years of negotiations China joined the WTO, and the so-called "Doha Round" of global trade negotiations was launched.

A decade later, the legacy of the Doha get-together is a good-news, bad-news story. The good news is that China has risen like a rocket in global trade and the country has accumulated remarkable wealth. The bad news is that WTO rules are proving to be ineffective in dealing with the wide range of discriminatory and distorting Chinese industrial policies, and the WTO is unable to modernize multilateral trade rules. And these two tales—China's remarkable rise and the WTO's rising dysfunction—are equal parts unconnected and intertwined.

At the time of the Doha meeting, China's share of world trade was between 3 and 4 percent. By 2010, that number had surpassed 10 percent. China was able to power through the 2008 global financial crisis that sent the United States, European Union, and other developed economies tumbling. Since joining the WTO, China has grown to become a financial powerhouse with global reach. (Just one example: the China Development Bank and Chinese Export-Import Bank issued more loans to developing countries in 2009–2010 than the World Bank.[185]) At the same time, China has become a master at playing along with the WTO processes and procedures while maneuvering through loopholes and privately but firmly warning countries and companies that filing WTO complaints and domestic trade remedy cases pursuant to WTO rules will bring retribution. As one senior trade attorney put it, "The current system only influences China to change in cosmetic ways. China gets the benefit of WTO membership but doesn't suffer the consequences."[186]

A quick look back provides perspective. When the World Bank and International Monetary Fund were founded in 1944, a parallel trade body was scuttled by the US Congress. Instead, the General Agreement on Tariffs and Trade (GATT) was signed in 1947 under United Nation auspices as the vehicle for managing trade.

GATT negotiations were eased by American predominance after World War II and Cold War competition that led the United States to reduce its tariffs and provide foreign aid without insisting on immediate reciprocity. The GATT power structure eroded as trade issues became more complex and trade volume grew. The end of fixed exchange rates, the oil shock, and the rise of Japan in the 1970s ended US domination of GATT negotiations. [187]

The rise of the Asian Tigers—South Korea, Taiwan, Hong Kong, and Singapore—ended a two-hundred-year trade pattern of poor countries exporting raw materials to the developed world which exported goods and services back to them. This contributed to the World Trade Organization supplanting GATT in January 1995 as the arbiter of global trade. From its founding, the WTO has been democratic. One country, one vote. Small and poor countries share an equal voice with the developed countries.

The measures adopted by the WTO to expand trade protocols beyond GATT's focus on physical products that cross borders include:

The Agreement on Trade-Related Aspects of Intellectual Property Rights (TRIPS), which aims to protect copyrights, industrial designs, patents, trademarks, and other forms of technological innovation.

The Agreement on Trade-Related Investment Measures (TRIMS), which seeks to prohibit trade-related investment measures such as local content requirements and forced technology transfers.

The General Agreement on Trade in Services (GATS), which addresses foreign investment in services and limits service business monopolies and exclusive service suppliers.

The Doha Round is the first global multilateral trade negotiation under the democratized WTO. In addition to 148 countries having an equal say, the WTO employs a "single-undertaking" procedure, which means "virtually every item of the negotiation is part of a whole and indivisible package and cannot be agreed separately."[188] In other words, nothing can be agreed until everything is agreed—by everybody.

Ten years after Doha began, WTO officials say the discussions are "at an impasse."[189] The impasse is a result of a variety of factors. China's principal emerging market competitors—Brazil and India—were clearly not ready to accept new WTO agreements which would have further opened their markets to China. The United States was not ready to accept proposed agreements for goods and services which did not open the emerging country markets. Of special significance, especially for the future, the Doha Round agenda does not include substantial changes to WTO rules which would address ongoing and anticipated problems caused by China's discriminatory and distorting industrial policies.

China is not sitting on the sidelines as the WTO system approaches paralysis and continually falls short in developing twenty-first-century rules. Analysts Aaditya Mattoo and Arvind Subramanian in a December 2011 study for the World Bank said that "a significant but publicly unacknowledged impediment to concluding the Doha negotiations is the WTO members' difficulty in coming to terms with China's trade juggernaut and the policies, such as the managed exchange rate, that are perceived to fuel it but are not part of the Doha agenda." [190]

China is a major factor because of the sheer size of its export machine and domestic economy, not to mention its speed of growth. China's system is so different that it is essentially incompatible with the WTO structure and procedures. China's judges and arbitrators are appointed by and supervised by Party officials. Unlike the judiciaries of most WTO members, Chinese courts lack the independence as well as the authority to compel evidence-gathering. This makes it nearly impossible for lawsuits and other legal actions to be employed in China to gather the detailed evidence required by the WTO dispute settlement bodies to adjudicate cases.

"To make a case in the WTO you need data. The standards are very high so you need a legal discovery process in order to gather evidence," said an American attorney who has been handling trade and business disputes involving China for nearly three decades. "The Chinese legal and political systems make it nearly impossible to gather the evidence."[191]

The Tangled Spaghetti Bowl of Trade

What economist Jagdish Bhagwati describes as a "spaghetti bowl" of trade agreements is emerging as the multilateral WTO system becomes increasingly weak. As of July 2010, a total of 474 country-to-country, situation-specific, and regional trade agreements had been notified to the WTO, though the WTO holds no regulatory control over them.

The United States and China are among the most active participants. Since 2001, the United States has worked out bilateral agreements with Australia, Bahrain, Chile, Colombia, Korea, Morocco, Oman, Peru, Singapore, and six countries in Central America. China has forged bilateral free trade agreements with ASEAN, Taiwan, Chile, New Zealand, Pakistan, Peru, and Singapore. It is working on deals with Japan, Korea, Costa Rica, Australia, Norway, and Switzerland.

In scrambling for solutions to China's trade juggernaut, trade attorneys are drafting language for future trade agreements to address such anti-competitive distortions as: predatory regulatory regimes; currency exchange rates; investment restrictions; subsidies, financing, and policy advantages provided to SOEs; anti-competitive standards and technical barriers to trade; anti-competitive tax policies; IP protection and enforcement; and access to critical minerals.

The Obama administration envisions the Trans-Pacific Partnership (TPP) to be a "twenty-first-century trade agreement" that incorporates these solutions. In September 2008, the United States announced its intent to begin negotiations with the original four signatories—Chile, New Zealand, Brunei, and Singapore—as well as Australia, Peru, and Vietnam. Malaysia, Japan, Canada, the Philippines, South Korea, Thailand, and Taiwan have expressed an interest in joining.

China has not asked to join the talks. Shen Minghui, a director at the Chinese Academy of Social Sciences' Institute of Asia-Pacific Studies, said that the proposed agreement, which includes new language aimed at achieving "competitive neutrality" between SOEs and private companies, "sets too high of a standard for free trade in goods and services in too short of a time."[192]

The Plodding Pursuit of Pyrrhic Victories

China is managing its WTO membership as if it were a giant Sino-foreign joint venture.

As with many of the joint ventures in China between SOEs and multinationals, China is getting its way in the WTO by employing such tried-and-true JV management techniques as intimidation, obfuscation, and the dispensation of favors when necessary. This behavior is most pronounced when the country's WTO commitments clash with Party priorities.

During the five-year period allotted for China to phase in its WTO commitments, China enacted many impressive and sweeping changes. The country reduced tariffs and nontariff barriers and expanded market access for other WTO members. Intellectual property regulations were strengthened, and government rulemaking was made more transparent. This helped US exports to China rise by some 380 percent between 2001 and 2010—to $92 billion from $19 billion. Cross-border trade in commercial services also grew rapidly, with services supplied by majority-US-owned firms in China totaling $23 billion by 2009.[193]

Upon joining in 2001, Chinese policymakers knew that the WTO was not comprehensive and that there would be opportunities to game the system. They also knew that they had to modernize the economy and couldn't do so alone. The country's WTO obligations lowered traditional trade barriers and brought a fresh onslaught of foreign investment. However, when the WTO grace period ended in 2006, China launched the Indigenous Innovation and SOE-strengthening policies, likely with the knowledge that there are no clear and effective WTO rules to discipline their use. The Chinese bureaucracy followed up with an array of licensing, certification, capital commitment, technical standards, technology transfer, and local content requirements to block market access and protect local companies. Many of these restrictions are inconsistent with WTO rules. But companies and countries are too frightened of retaliation to file complaints.

"After 2006, as China's progress toward further market liberalization began to slow . . . in some instances Chinese policymakers showed little appreciation of the carefully negotiated conditions for China's WTO accession that were designed to lead to significantly reduced levels of trade-distorting government policies," the USTR reported to Congress in

December 2011. "In fact, in recent years, China seems to be embracing state capitalism more strongly, rather than continuing to move toward the economic reform goals that originally drove its pursuit of WTO membership."[194]

The December 2011 World Bank Study's Appraisal

China's IPR regime: "A case of possible violation of the letter of WTO law."

China's currency policy: "A case of violating the spirit of the WTO law."

China's services trade regime: "Inhabiting the murky ground in between."

China's export restrictions: "Inconsistent with China's accession commitments."[201]

As is often the case with Sino-foreign joint ventures, China had decided it wanted better terms than in the original agreement. Chinese government entities and SOEs usually don't renegotiate deals they've grown to dislike. Instead, they ignore the parts that don't work for the Chinese side, and vigorously enforce the clauses that do. When foreign partners ask questions, the Chinese partner simply talks in circles. Ancient and obscure parables are often preferred. If the foreigners threaten legal action, they are reminded that the Chinese side holds a huge hammer. No matter the ownership percentages of the joint venture, the Chinese side owns 100 percent of the political power and influence with the regulators that allow foreigners to do business in China.

Sometimes these "reminders" are none-too-subtle warnings. When foreign governments and multinationals loudly complained about Indigenous Innovation several years ago, various Chinese ministries invited senior executives for discussions. After one such meeting, a vice minister buttonholed an American multinational boss and asked, "Are you a Chinese company?" meaning, are you registered in China? When the executive answered, "Yes, of course," the Vice-Minister responded, "Then, start acting like one!" In other words, do what you are told.[195]

The strategy of winning through intimidation is working well for China. Foreign companies are aware that any support for trade actions against China—even behind the scenes—will negatively impact their businesses. Country representatives to the WTO all know that a vote against China can come back to haunt them. China seldom forgives and never forgets. Threats of retribution are either passed along directly in private meetings or in smiling asides at banquets and receptions. These practices are so pervasive that senior American and European officials and business associations are complaining publicly.

The Chinese government "has retaliated against individual EU member states in relation to political issues or activities in the EU by severing diplomatic relations, excluding companies from public procurement projects or withdrawing business licenses in China," the trade group BUSINESS EUROPE said in October 2011. [196]

In March, the European Union disclosed for the first time it is contemplating filing trade cases even if companies don't file complaints. "We are following a number of cases and . . . what we see is, yes, companies are intimidated," EU Trade Commissioner Karel De Gucht told the *Wall Street Journal.* "What we have to do is protect the European interest. We will not accept governments putting pressure on our companies."[197]

China has been unusually direct in warning of retribution for the European Union's Emissions Trading System (ETS). Starting this year, ETS requires airlines operating at any EU airport to purchase carbon credits to offset their carbon dioxide emissions. Airbus executives say that as a result China is withholding final approval on contracts for forty-five Airbus jetliners valued at $12 billion. China's Ambassador to the European Union Wu Hailong pulled no punches when asked about this in March. Ambassador Wu told the *Wall Street Journal* that with Chinese airlines included in the ETS, "it makes sense for them to go to Boeing." Ambassador Wu added that ETS "could lead to a long-term conflict and could lead to retaliation." Mr. Wu said that Chinese airplane orders are "largely a commercial decision by the airline, but of course their decision will be influenced by the position of the central government on ETS."[198]

In a November 2011 speech at an event in Geneva marking China's tenth anniversary as a WTO member, US Ambassador to the WTO Michael Punke was as direct as a diplomat can be:

> Before concluding our review of China's first 10 years of WTO membership, one other aspect of China's conduct as a WTO member needs to be highlighted and discussed, and that is the perception among WTO members that Chinese government authorities at times use intimidation as a trade tool. China's trading partners have heard from their enterprises on too many occasions that Chinese regulatory authorities threaten to withhold necessary approval or take other retaliatory actions against foreign enterprises if they speak out against problematic Chinese policies or are perceived as responding cooperatively to their governments' efforts to challenge them.[199]

In its "US Trade and Investment Policy" study last year, the Council on Foreign Relations placed the dispute settlement system at the top of its list of the WTO's "significant shortcomings," noting the "long time required to bring and resolve cases so that even a favorable ruling may be a pyrrhic victory because the economic damage has already been done."[200]

Delay, Distract, and Dominate

Despite the outcry over Indigenous Innovation, American multinationals often run for cover when the US Trade Representative asks for help in filing a WTO case. In one case, it took four years and an organization with no presence in China to get the ball rolling. The United Steelworkers (USW) in September 2010 stepped forward with a 5,800-page petition. The filing detailed a soup-to-nuts list of unfair practices in the clean-tech sector, from technology transfer requirements to restrictions on critical materials to massive subsidies for SOEs.

The USTR responded in December with a WTO petition focused on wind power. The case was settled in June 2011 before the WTO established a dispute settlement panel. China agreed to eliminate a subsidy program for wind-turbine manufacturers. A 70 percent local-content requirement for wind turbines purchased by Chinese power generators had been scrapped in July 2009 after four years of US-China talks. The requirement clearly violated WTO rules. The lengthy discussions provided Chinese companies the time needed to dominate the sector.[202]

In 2004, foreign wind turbines accounted for 75 percent of the Chinese market. By 2010, Chinese producers supplied more than 85 percent of the local market.[203] The major beneficiaries of the local content requirement were the SOEs, which have a 90 percent market share in China's wind power farms.[204]

Extra Rare with a Side of Scarcity

China's September 2010 restrictions on rare earth exports to Japan during a territorial dispute over the Diaoyu/Senkaku Islands sent a chill down the spine of the global technology community. China produces 97 percent of the world supply of these 17 elements that are essential for making everything from solar panels to batteries to smartphones to guided missiles and jet engines.

Once China cut exports of rare earths to Japan, analysts discovered that despite fierce global demand, Chinese exports of these elements had declined to 30,000 tons in 2010 from about 47,000 tons in 2000.[205] In 2011, as domestic production totaled 120,000 tons, China reserved 87,000 tons for domestic use.[206] The restrictions fueled the quadrupling of average global prices between 2010 and 2011. Neodymium, of which one kilogram goes into a Toyota Prius, increased to $283 per kilo from $42. Samarium, crucial for missiles, climbed to $147 per kilo from $18.50.[207] Abundant supply in China kept prices lower and incentivized companies to move manufacturing to China.

Zhao Shuanglian, the vice chairman of the Inner Mongolia Autonomous Region (home to 75 percent of China's rare earth deposits), publicly highlighted this opportunity in September 2009 after MIIT issued a draft policy for tightening rare earth exports. Noting that the elements are "the most important resource for Inner Mongolia," Zhao said the government wanted to "attract users of rare earths to set up in Inner Mongolia" for manufacturing.[208]

In March 2012 the United States, European Union, and Japan filed separate and simultaneous WTO cases. Joined by a dozen other WTO members, their petitions allege WTO violations of export duties, export quotas, export pricing requirements, as well as related export procedures and requirements on rare earths. "In all, China's export restraints on the materials at issue in this dispute cover more than 100 tariff codes," the USTR said. "China committed as part of

(continued on next page)

the terms of its WTO accession to eliminate export duties for all products other than those listed in a specific annex. The export duties the United States is challenging are imposed on products not listed in that annex."[209]

China has responded by citing a decades-old GATT legal exception that allows export restrictions aimed at "conserving a scarce natural resource or protecting the environment."[210] In January 2012, despite making this same argument, China lost a similar case. In question were bauxite, coke, fluorspar, magnesium, manganese, and a number of other raw materials of which China is the top global supplier. Even if China loses the rare earth cases, the country has bought precious time. China is working to create unified pricing, transportation, and sales systems for rare earths by consolidating production into three to five SOE national champion conglomerates. This SOE control of the industry would allow the government to restrict output by fiat, thereby nullifying any adverse WTO ruling.[211]

Mutual Interests Not Previously Recognized

Since China joined the WTO, American negotiators have found themselves in an increasingly weak position. They are largely relegated to employing the power of persuasion in bilateral dialogues to convince China to make changes, arguing—seldom with result—that such changes would be in China's own interest.

The United States hasn't always lacked leverage in matters of trade. Until the WTO was established in 1995, the United States employed an array of effective tools. Section 301 of the 1974 trade act allowed the president to order unilateral trade sanctions to combat discriminatory policies of trading partners. The Section 301 mechanism was used as a threat against China several times in the 1990s, prior to its WTO membership, to achieve broad market access and IPR protection agreements. The United States essentially gave up its right in the WTO Uruguay Round to use

Section 301 except in those cases where there are neither international rules nor international dispute settlement provisions. When China joined the WTO in 2001, the country came under this protective WTO umbrella. As a result, the United States has been unable to deploy the trade tools used previously against Japan, China, and others.

Even when WTO cases are filed, the elaborate preparation required and the time-consuming WTO process itself allow China to achieve its objectives long before any rulings. The previously referenced case brought against China UnionPay is just one example. Another is a 2006 WTO case involving Chinese restrictions on imported auto parts. The United States, European Union, and Canada won the case. But in the interim China was able to further develop its indigenous suppliers and supply chain.[212]

US officials are increasingly frustrated by endless "dialogues" with their Chinese counterparts who, well aware that actual negotiation is optional, simply run out the clock. "In summary, each of the traditional trade enforcement tools used by the United States is either no longer available or no longer particularly effective," said the Council on Foreign Relations trade task force. "As the world's biggest market, the United States had more power than any other country to get its way in trade disputes by threating to block imports, and thus had much to lose by foreclosing that option."[213]

American politicians love to point the finger at China's exchange rate to explain this state of overreliance. Yet American policymakers and Congress have handed China a gift by spending so many years haranguing China to revalue its currency. While China's artificially low exchange rate has historically been viewed by some as an unfair trade advantage, it is a mere droplet in the ocean of industrial policies that China employs. And many of these are far more harmful to American interests than a currency peg that allows American consumers to enjoy unusually cheap prices on Chinese-made goods, most of them produced in factories that left American soil long ago.

The key dialogues between the United States and China have devolved to the point of US officials presenting economic studies and other evidence to try to persuade China that there are better ways to do things. Because the US market is already wide open to Chinese products, US negotiators have no bargaining chips left. As the Council on Foreign Relations trade study put it, "A fundamental purpose of such negotiations is to find mutual interests not previously recognized."[214]

The US-China Strategic & Economic Dialogue in May this year did produce a few understandings regarding SOEs that could serve as a basis for further discussions. China said it would steadily increase the dividends that SOEs pay to the government—and that technology transfer and technology cooperation are not to be used as a pre-condition for market access. "The Chinese Government commits to developing a market environment of fair competition for enterprises of all kinds of ownership and to providing non-discriminatory treatment for enterprises of all kinds of ownership in terms of credit provision, taxation incentives, and regulatory policies," the S&ED joint fact sheet said. "The United States welcomes business investment from all countries, including China, and including from state-owned enterprises."[215]

Process Versus Outcomes

Since the global financial crisis, there has been an ever-increasing perception, both inside and outside the US government, that China seems to be only going through the motions in trade and investment forums.[216]

One clear example is the Joint Commission on Commerce and Trade (JCCT) annual meeting. Established in 1983, this forum, led by the US secretary of commerce, the US trade representative, and a Chinese vice premier, is the highest level bilateral trade dialogue between the two countries. The JCCT annual meeting, which alternates between Washington and Beijing, includes participants from dozens of ministries and agencies from both governments. As of August 2011, the JCCT had sixteen active working groups covering a wide variety of issues and industries, including intellectual property, environment, information industry, pharmaceutical and medical devices, statistics, commercial law, and trade and investment.[217]

While the JCCT remains an important forum for face-to-face talk between US and Chinese officials, the same issues are discussed year after year, resulting in the same promised remedies.

All government-to-government meetings must result in "deliverables." The headliners from the most recent JCCT meeting, in November 2011 in Chengdu, were:[218]

- **Electric Vehicles:** China "does not and will not" mandate the transfer of technology and "will not impose any requirements for foreign-invested companies to establish domestic brands in China." (Foreign automakers are already producing Chinese brands after being verbally instructed by Chinese officials that any manufacturing expansion approvals would be contingent on doing that.)[219]

- **Government and SOE Use of Pirated Software:** China will make permanent a "State Council leadership structure" addressing IPR issues to "enhance its ability to crack down on IPR infringement." China also will "continue to take measures to ensure that governments at all levels use only legitimate software, ensuring that all the types of software used by government agencies are licensed." (In 2004, China agreed to extend an existing ban on the use of pirated software in central and provincial government agencies, to include local governments. China again made this pledge in 2005, vowing to complete the legalization program by the end of that year. In November 2005, the government announced that it had found no pirated software on government office computers. In a 2006 JCCT IPR working group meeting, China reaffirmed its prior commitments to ensure the use of legal software at all levels of government and adopt procedures to ensure that enterprises use legal software, beginning with SOEs and other large enterprises. In April of that year, China announced that at least four Chinese manufacturers had signed agreements to purchase and pre-install US operating system software. The no-piracy policy was reiterated in China's 2007 and 2008 IPR Action Plans, though not in its 2009 plan.)[220]

- **Indigenous Innovation Procurement Requirements:** China said that governments of provinces, municipalities, and autonomous regions would eliminate "any catalogs or other measures linking innovation policies to government procurement preferences." (China cleared the way for this by establishing an exception process. For a government unit to purchase foreign products, the unit must consult customs and other agencies and write a report. An expert committee of at least five officials then reviews the purchase request documentation. This all has to be documented online so that local competitors can make certain they have a chance of supplying the product, making the process highly public. Submitting these requests to purchase foreign products is therefore not considered a smart path to political advancement in China.)[221]

The frustration on both sides is illustrated by the snail's-pace progress on China joining the WTO Government Procurement Agreement (GPA), a plurilateral agreement designed to prevent countries from using government procurement to discriminate against foreign products. This is important from the US perspective because, according to a recent European Chamber of Commerce study, government procurement accounts for 20 percent of China's GDP.

Though China committed to joining the GPA "as soon as possible" upon its 2001 WTO accession, only in 2007 did China submit its initial GPA offer, which GPA members considered inadequate. In 2008, China agreed to submit an improved offer. This new offer, made in July 2010, was again rejected. China promised an improved offer by the end of 2011. That deadline was not met.[222]

A key point of dispute is the inclusion of procurement by SOEs. The United States insists that this is a prerequisite for any deal. China is unwilling to concede because SOE purchasing is considered a major driver of China's industrial policies. Eleven years on, discussions about China's accession are nowhere close to satisfying either side, and China is largely going through the motions in its offers to accede.

When speaking privately, some Chinese officials acknowledge that their interest in these bilateral dialogues is indeed fading—due largely to the preeminence of central government priorities. Every year, China faces the same litany of requests from the United States on issues that both sides know they can't move on until the Party's overarching objectives have been achieved. These include flashpoint topics like rare earth minerals, IPR, the dollar-yuan exchange rate, and many others. As one Chinese official said in a recent interview, "We just have different understandings of these things."[223]

What is at work here is a serious US-China disconnect. "Americans focus on the process more than the substance," a veteran US trade negotiator said in an interview. "It is always about due process; is this fair, are people following the rules. The Chinese don't focus on process, they focus on outcomes. The US system focuses on process. If the process is followed, then you have to accept the results."

The US government may have already ceded too much ground for it to matter much. US multinationals face a catch-22 in China. Since the global financial crisis and the resulting US and EU recessions, the multinationals are more reliant on the China market than ever before. They also face Chinese retaliation if they support WTO cases and other trade actions. So multinational executives all too often have little choice but to cut deals to provide Chinese SOEs with technology in exchange for a presence in the expanding China market. These companies are well aware that this exchange could make these SOEs future global competitors, backed by state subsidies that are impossible to compete against. But the China market is too big to bypass.

In May this year, however, the EU Chamber of Commerce in China released a survey indicating that some EU companies are contemplating reducing their exposure in China. "Due to market access and regulatory barriers, 48 percent of European companies report missing out on business opportunities, with 64 percent of these estimating the value of these missed opportunities to represent 10–50 percent of revenue," the Chamber survey stated, adding that "22 percent of respondents admitted that they are considering shifting investment from China to other markets."[224]

A prominent American trade attorney called today's situation with China—the discriminatory trade and investment policies as well as the use of forced technology transfers and trade-secret theft—"America's biggest challenge since the Cold War."[225]

"The United States is being massively outmaneuvered and the government doesn't even see it," he said in an interview. "There are individuals in the government who understand this. But the government as a whole doesn't see the big picture. The business community can't carry this issue in DC. Various industries and individual companies are split because of their dependence on the China market and how China can either buy them off or intimidate them. The national security community has to get behind this to protect the integrity of the US technology base even if no company is complaining at all."

CHAPTER FIVE

REENGINEERING THE CHINA MODEL

Senior Party leaders and key policymakers say that continued success requires fundamental and far-reaching reforms. The question is whether nationalist ideologues and powerful vested interests enriched by the current system are sufficiently entrenched to continue blocking the way forward.

Heroically Transcending the Existing International System

To outsiders, China's new nationalism appears to have shifted from insecurity to anger and aggression. This is a byproduct of the Party's unswerving focus on its own survival. Trumping any international considerations is the belief that the Party could lose control of China if it doesn't command the country's banks and other major economic actors through SOEs.

"Genuine integration into the global liberal order would demand significant modifications to the Chinese political economy—and to how China is ruled—that could fatally weaken the relevance of the CCP and fundamentally threaten the Party's tenuous bargain with China's economic and social elites," the *American Interest* said in a June 2012 essay. "Since retaining power remains the CCP's paramount priority, Chinese economic entities, especially those directly owned by the state, remain latent tools not just of statecraft but also of regime security within its evolved 'Leninist worldview.'"[226]

Not that China's leaders are likely feeling much pressure to level the playing field, given the proven effectiveness of their policies of bullying trade partners. In fact, this success has given rise to a sort of casual nationalist chauvinism against the United States that is frequently captured in the Chinese media. Since the onset of the global financial crisis, media outlets and many Chinese scholars have been touting the decline of America and the superiority of the China Model. The 2009 best seller *Unhappy China* fueled this view with its assertion that the crisis "reflects the decay and collapse of American society."

As this fall's Chinese leadership transition approaches, the Party itself is striking back strongly against any criticism. This was abundantly clear after the Honolulu Asia-Pacific Economic Cooperation (APEC) meetings in November 2011, when US President Barack Obama criticized China for "gaming the system." Obama called on Chinese leaders to acknowledge that the country has "grown up" and must "understand that their role is different now than it might have been twenty years ago or thirty years ago when if they were breaking some rules it didn't really matter, it didn't have a significant impact."[227] An editorial in *People's Daily* responded by saying "the rules of the game are not timeless" and the West is failing to recognize that "the world is changing." The editorial went on to say, "There's a difficult road from recognizing a change in eras to adjusting to that change. Smart people move with the times, conceited people are eliminated by history."[228]

Party operatives who head up dominant SOEs can be even more direct. AVIC Chairman Lin Zuoming said recently that reforms constitute a foreign conspiracy to weaken the Party. "In this new era, there are two important forces supporting the foundations of the ruling Party. One is having the People's Liberation Army, and one is maintaining the state-owned part of the economy," the *Nanjing Daily* quoted Lin as saying at an April meeting of AVIC Party members. "When the state-owned economy has collapsed, the enemies will then seek the army's collapse. Privatizing the economy and taking away the Party's control of the army by nationalizing the military are conspiracies by international enemies to shake the base of the ruling Party."[229]

On the flip side of Lin's paranoia is the belief that China has built a unique and successful model. No small number of Chinese scholars, journalists, and Party apparatchiks are now asserting that China should shake off the influence of the West and become a "heroic state" capable of "transcending the existing international system."[230]

Yet China isn't the first country to build global economic power through expedient industrial policies and protectionism. Back in 1721, British Prime Minister Robert Walpole established a system of protecting British manufacturing through high tariffs on imported goods, subsidies for exports, and forbidding British colonies from exporting goods that competed with British manufacturers. These basic policies remained in place until 1860.[231]

America's founders learned Walpole's lessons well. Alexander Hamilton, the first US treasury secretary, championed similar policies in his 1791 report to Congress in which he coined the term "infant industries." In detailing policies to protect "industries in their infancy," Hamilton proposed protective tariffs, import bans, subsidies for encouraged industries, export bans on key raw materials, prizes and patents for inventions, the regulation of product standards, and the development of infrastructure for finance and transportation. "Hamilton provided the blueprint for US economic policy until the end of the Second World War," wrote Cambridge University economist Ha-Joon Chang in his 2008 book *Bad Samaritans*. "His infant industry program created the conditions for rapid industrial development."[232]

The tight web of protectionist policies under Japan's Ministry of International Trade and Industry (MITI) provided a blueprint for what is occurring in China today. Party scholars translated Chalmers Johnson's book *MITI and the Japanese Miracle* into Chinese in September 1992. This led to China's 1994 "Outline for Industrial Policy" that echoed MITI's 1960s designation of electronics, machinery, petrochemicals, automobiles, and construction as pillar industries.

Japan's inability to unwind these policies has contributed to that country's long period of economic stagnation. On the other hand, for the United States and many others, moving beyond protectionism and mercantilism was essential for reaching the ranks of high-income societies.

Stuck in the Middle

It has been fun while it's lasted. But China's days of rapid development through mercantilism and protectionism may be coming to an end. The China Model is facing a growing set of contradictions that threaten to undermine it. The incredible wealth accumulated by the Party and business elite threatens to ensnare the country in what economists call the middle-income trap.

The middle-income trap argument goes something like this: when an emerging economy's fast-development model of low-cost labor and easy technology adoption maxes out the benefit of these competitive advantages, the country will be unable to sustain significant economic and social progress unless it embraces new drivers of growth. The advantages of low-cost labor disappear as the country reaches middle-income levels, and wage growth expansion threatens the competitiveness of exports. Similarly, the productivity gains realized through rapid adoption of borrowed technology dry up eventually without new sources of innovation. Without the rise of a domestic consumer base to offset export decline and drive growth—

typically through innovation—the emerging economy will languish in the middle-income range, unable to produce the value that supports continued wage growth.

This topic was addressed head-on in the DRC–World Bank "China 2030" report. "The concept of a middle-income trap has some empirical backing," notes the report. "Latin America and the Middle East provide compelling support for the trap hypothesis: in these two regions, most economies reached middle-income status as early as the 1960s and 1970s and have remained there ever since." The report says that in 1960 there were 101 middle-income economies. By 2008, however, only 13 of them had reached high-income status.[233]

With the rural underemployed labor force continuing to shrink and wage growth picking up at a rapid clip, China has unquestionably reached this turning point. The DRC–World Bank paper predicts China can achieve the 6.6 percent average annual growth for the next twenty years necessary to avoid the trap if the government embarks on a host of reforms listed in the report.

Targeting GDP is the easy part. Much more difficult is conceptualizing the magnitude of reform that must take place to support such growth. In many ways, China's success relies on transforming the downtrodden and dispossessed migrant workers into the backbone of China's domestic consumption economy. The government must now recast these migrant workers as full urban citizens and accord them the social benefits necessary for them to participate fully in the economy.

Similarly, the decades of productivity growth driven by assimilating, absorbing, and re-innovating foreign technology are nearing an end. "If countries cannot increase productivity through innovation (rather than continuing to rely on foreign technology) they find themselves trapped," the DRC–World Bank study states.

These challenges are made even more urgent by the fact that China is approaching the end of its demographic dividend. The birth boom of the 1960s and 1970s provided the enormous low-cost factory workforce for the 1990s and 2000s. But between 2010 and 2020 the number of available workers between the ages of twenty and twenty-four, the core of China's factory workforce, will decline by nearly 50 percent. China is also destined to get old before it gets rich. In 2010, 115 million Chinese were aged sixty-five or older. This number is projected to swell to 240 million by 2030. And by 2030, some one-quarter of men in their late thirties will never have married. With a birth ratio of 120 boys to 100 girls, this imbalance is only expected to get worse.

The Chinese government must worry about unrest among the urban elite if the number of white-collar jobs is insufficient. From 2000 to 2010, China increased its university population from 6 million students to 30 million, while annual graduates increased from 2 million to 6.5 million. The number of college graduates is estimated to increase by 200 million over the next two decades —more than the entire labor force of the United States.[234]

Breakthrough Progress to a Market of Unprecedented Size

China can't make it to the next stage of development without essentially turning its social and economic model upside down—while radically changing the way reforms are carried out.

To create an urban middle class from the current mass of migrant workers, China will need to go beyond its customary step-by-step modifications and launch comprehensive reforms of the country's economic, financial, social, cultural, and political systems—and do so simultaneously and at all levels of government and society. This is the underlying message of the current Twelfth Five-Year Plan, as well as the DRC–World Bank "China 2030" study.

Just over 50 percent of the Chinese population now lives in cities, compared with less than 20 percent when reforms began thirty years ago. By 2030, some two-thirds of China's people are expected to be living in cities. This means that an average of 13 million to 15 million rural residents will move to cities each year, the equivalent of adding the population of Tokyo to urban areas in China annually.

In 2011, an estimated 252 million farm workers were employed in cities, with 158 million of them classified by the government as "migrant workers" as they left local regions for jobs in distant cities. These migrant workers—nearly equal to the combined population of Britain, Spain, and Italy—primarily work in manufacturing, construction, and the service industry. In contrast to earlier waves of migrants, the current generation is China's first to be firmly non-agricultural, as 90 percent of them have never as much as set foot in the fields. They are also young, having left home at an average age of seventeen. The typical migrant works nine hours a day, six days a week for RMB 1,800 ($280) a month. Two-thirds live in factory dorms or on building sites, while others rent rooms in villages on the outskirts of cities. What they also have in common is access during their countryside upbringing to satellite TV shows depicting the luxurious lives of the urban rich. As a result, "even relative poverty is becoming hard for people to accept,"[235] said Liu He, the deputy director of the DRC and a key adviser to top Party leaders.

Perhaps the most challenging and perplexing reforms will be fixing the *hukou* (housing registration) system enacted in the 1950s to prevent peasants from flooding into the cities. As of 2009, the government estimates that more than a quarter of urban residents don't have an urban *hukou*—and therefore lack access to the social support associated with legal city residency, including health care and education.[236] Migrant children who accompany their parents to cities study in shanty schools set up by the migrants themselves. An estimated fifty-eight million children—nearly a quarter of China's children—are left behind in the villages to be cared for by the elderly. "The youngsters face stark psychological and emotional challenges; many struggle to keep up with their lessons and end up abandoning school in their teens to join their parents on the road," social researchers told the *Los Angeles Times*."[237]

Liu He provided a guide to the Chinese government's thinking in an April 2011 report titled "The Basic Logic Behind the Twelfth Five-Year Plan."[238] He emphasized that housing registration reform is an essential element of the "progress of a breakthrough nature" necessary for China to continue to move ahead. He suggested that if ten million farmers can be transformed into real urbanites per year, they will form a "potential new global market of unprecedented size." For this to happen, Liu said, migrants must achieve "personal balance sheets" in which job opportunities, take-home pay, and cost of living allow them to live well. The goal, he added, would be for each migrant to become "a true urbanite, joining the ranks of modern civilization as opposed to somebody who lives like a migratory bird."

China's economic structure is no less imbalanced than its social one. Monopoly SOEs dominate sector after sector, but they contribute almost nothing to overall employment and economic growth. China has incredible scientific talent and a dire need to become a country that creates technological innovation, but the web of industrial policies aimed at innovation is mostly sparking creative corruption.

One baseline policy that must be reversed to drive innovation is relaxing of the state stranglehold on private enterprise. For this to happen, the hegemony enjoyed by the Big Four state banks has to be broken. The SOE sector will have to be slimmed down and sidelined. Financing for private business must be made widely available. And transparency and rule of law will need to gradually replace political repression and information suppression as the mechanisms for handling China's debilitating and endemic corruption.

Both the "China 2030" study and the Twelfth Five-Year Plan portray these massive shifts as make-or-break objectives for the country.

Officials are signaling that the Deng Xiaoping era is truly over in two major ways. In the first place, Chinese leaders have amended Deng's "low profile" directive for global political and commercial affairs to instead be "active" and assertive. During a Party meeting in July 2009, President Hu told several hundred top leaders to be more "assertive" in their dealings with foreigners and foreign countries. He enshrined this in Party liturgy by adjusting Deng's foreign policy guideline that had been issued in 1989 after the collapse of the communist Eastern bloc. President Hu added two characters to Deng's eight-character slogan: *taoguang yanghui, yousuo zuowei* (Keep a low profile and bide our time, while getting something accomplished). The word *jiji,* or "actively," was added to make it "while actively getting something accomplished."[239]

The second revision to Deng's guiding precepts involves domestic policy. China can no longer depend on Deng's gradualist style of reform. As Shaanxi province Governor Zhao Zhengyong put it during the National People's Congress in March, "At first, reform was about crossing the river by feeling the stones. We adjusted to whatever problems arose. But we've reached a stage where we can't continue in this manner. Now, we need comprehensive reform and need to consider the whole system."

Liu He echoes Zhao's sentiments in advocating an all-hands-on-deck approach to replace the "operate from the top downwards" reforms of the past. "The goals and the structure of systems must be designed at the top level, while public consensus in support of deepening reform must be generated through mobilizing all members of society," Liu wrote.

The Twelfth Five-Year Plan represents a reset, creating a model that moves away from overreliance on investments and exports and toward consumption-led growth. Chinese consumption is now only 35 percent of GDP. That compares with 71 percent in the US, 63 percent in Brazil, and 54 percent in India. The "China 2030" study estimates that for every 1 percent increase in China's urban population, there is a 1.4 percent increase in national consumption, creating a direct impact on GDP of 0.4 percent.

Liu He compares China's situation to drivers caught in in a tunnel traffic jam. As long as the cars are inching ahead, drivers won't be overly agitated. If traffic stops, however, people will lose patience and chaos could ensue. Liu He said "the rational approach" for Chinese reform, like managing traffic in a tunnel, is to "preserve order and gradually change the situation."

Unstable, Unbalanced, Uncoordinated, and Unsustainable

The Twelfth Five-Year Plan changes the previous slogan of "Strong State, Wealthy People" to "Wealthy People, Strong State." This implies that "wealthy people" is now the greater priority. But it also points to the major impediment to China's continued progress: the grip of political gridlock.

After ten years in power, Premier Wen is exiting the stage with constant curtain calls for political, economic, and social reforms—basically, promoting the agenda that is enshrined in "China 2030." He first introduced his "unstable, unbalanced, uncoordinated, and unsustainable" mantra in

2007. In the past couple of years he has expanded the recitation to include calls for the Party's power to be reduced. "A ruling Party's most important duty is to follow the constitution and the law, and restrict its activities within the constitution and the law," he told the 2011 World Economic Forum in Davos, Switzerland. "This requires changes in the use of the Party as a substitute for the government and in the phenomenon of over-concentration of power. For this, we need to reform the leadership system of the Party and the country."

The premier's remarks of this sort are often censored in China by the Party's internal security and propaganda authorities. These groups are now scrambling to dig a firebreak around the money-and-murder saga involving former Chongqing Party Secretary Bo Xilai, his wife Gu Kailai, and their extended families. But more than a few of China's estimated four hundred million micro-bloggers are focused on exposing the soul-searing corruption and mind-boggling wealth among the politically connected. Nobody knows whether or when this push-pull tussle will bring to a close China's decade-plus era that closely resembles America's robber baron era and Gilded Age—although compressed, compounded, and intensified.

A major obstacle to change is that the Party of the proletariat has become the Party of plutocrats. Jiang Zemin marked the Party's eightieth birthday in 2001 by opening membership to business people to represent "the most advanced productivity" and the "most advanced culture." Due to this and the strengthening of SOEs in the following decade, as of 2011 nearly one-quarter of the Party's eighty million members were "enterprise managers or professionals" while those designated as workers had dropped to seven million.[240]

Members of China's National People's Congress have become so wealthy that their meetings may best take place in a bank vault. According to a *Bloomberg* study, the wealthiest 70 NPC members are more than ten times richer than the top 660 officials in the US government. The combined worth of these NPC tycoons is about $90 billion (RMB 565.8 billion), while the combined wealth of the 535 members of the US Congress, the president and his cabinet, and the Supreme Court is $7.5 billion.[241]

The term "black-collar class" has become a popular appellation for SOE bosses and managers. Directly evoking their black company cars (ebony Audis are standard issue), the phrase also reflects the widely held belief that their lifestyle involves earning black money, having black fun, and keeping black secrets. The details of most corruption cases are covered up by the propaganda apparatus. But in this digital era, statistics and stories are increasingly difficult to hide. Take for instance the internal report on capital flight the People's Bank of China made public in 2011. The report, complied three years earlier, cited a Chinese Academy of Social Sciences study that claimed some eighteen thousand Party, government, police, courts, and SOE officials had absconded overseas with some RMB 800 billion ($127 billion) in government money since the mid-1990s. That's an average of about $7 million each. The report disappeared from the Internet within days.

China's reforms have unusually high stakes. Turning back to historical generalization, it is usually the intransigence of the elites that prevents countries from breaking through to high-income status. Those who get rich during the years of development—often through political connections and corruption—are usually the major roadblock to reform. Reforms threaten their financial fortunes, and leave them vulnerable politically, just as the middle class gains power and pushes for transparency and rule of law.

Sinologist Minxin Pei estimates that reforms recommended by the "China 2030" study could threaten five million Party jobs at SOEs and an equal number at government agencies that depend on strong state control of the economy. "World Bank–style reforms would jeopardize probably close to ten million official sinecures," Pei wrote after the study was published. "There is little doubt that reducing the SOEs' power would make the Chinese economy far more efficient and dynamic. But it is hard to imagine that a one-party regime would be willing to destroy its political base."[242]

"China 2030" estimates that China's global trade market share could grow to 20 percent by 2030, nearly double Japan's peak in the 1980s. With China's economy locked in tandem with the global one, the success or failure of China's reforms will reverberate throughout the world.

At the onset of the Global Financial Crisis, when China's new nationalism began to flower, a smug ditty zipped around the Chinese Internet, reflecting the sharp attitude shift in China at the time. "In the year of 1949, only socialism can save China. In the year of 1979, only capitalism can save China. In the year of 1989, only China can save socialism. In the year of 2009, only China can save capitalism."

In the years ahead, only by retooling the China Model can China reach "the future commanding heights."

APPENDIX:
ACRONYMS USED IN THE REPORT

AMCs	Asset Management Companies
AML	Anti-Monopoly Law
AMSC	American Superconductor Corp
APEC	Asia-Pacific Economic Cooperation
AVIC	Aviation Industry Corporation of China
CAAC	Civil Aviation Administration of China
CASS	Chinese Academy of Social Sciences
Chalco	Aluminum Corporation of China
CNOOC	China National Offshore Oil Corporation
Comac	Commercial Aircraft Corporation of China
CPA	Certified Public Accounts
DRC	Development Research Center
EU	European Union
EUCCC	European Union Chamber of Commerce in China
FBI	Federal Bureau of Investigation
GATS	General Agreement on Trade in Services
GATT	General Agreement on Tariffs and Trade
GDP	Gross Domestic Product
GPA	Government Procurement Agreement
ICBC	Industrial and Commercial Bank of China
IP	Intellectual Property
IPO	Initial Public Offering
IPR	Intellectual Property Right
IPTV	Internet Protocol TV
JCCT	Joint Commission on Commerce and Trade
JV	Joint Venture
MIIT	Ministry of Industry and Information Technology
MITI	Ministry of International Trade and Industry
MOF	Ministry of Finance

MOR	Ministry of Railways
MOST	Ministry of Science and Technology
NBS	National Bureau of Statistics
NDRC	National Development and Reform Commission
NEV	New Energy Vehicles
NPC	National People's Congress
NPL	non-performing-loans
NYSE	New York Stock Exchange
OECD	Organization for Economic Co-operation and Development
PBOC	People's Bank of China
PCAOB	Public Company Accounting Oversight Board
R&D	Research and Development
RoHS	Restriction of Hazardous Substances
SARFT	State Administration of Radio, Film, and Television
SASAC	State-owned Assets Supervision and Administration Commission
SEC	Securities and Exchange Commission
SEI	Strategic Emerging Industries
Sinopec	China Petroleum & Chemical Corporation
SOE	State-owned Enterprise
TPP	Trans-Pacific Partnership
TRIMS	The Agreement on Trade-Related Investment Measures
TRIPS	The Agreement on Trade Related Aspects of Intellectual Property Rights
TVEs	Township and Village Enterprises
USCC	US-China Economic and Security Review Commission
USCBC	US-China Business Council
USTR	United States Trade Representative
USW	United Steelworkers
WTO	World Trade Organization

ENDNOTES

[1] Justin Yifu Lin, "Speech: Demystifying the Chinese Economy," World Bank, Cambridge University Press, November 2011. http://siteresources.worldbank.org/DEC/Resources/84797-1104785060319 /598886-1104852366603/599473-1223731755312/Speech-on-Demystifying-the-Chinese-Economy.pdf.

[2] He Liu, "The Basic Logic Behind the 12th Five-Year Plan," State Council Development Research Center, published by China Development Research Foundation. http://www.cdrf.org.cn/plus/view.php?aid=279.

[3] Andrew Szamosszegi and Cole Kyle, "An Analysis of State-owned Enterprises and State Capitalism in China." October 26, 2011. US-China Economic and Security Review Commission (USCC): 8. http://www.uscc.gov/researchpapers/2011/10_26_11_CapitalTradeSOEStudy.pdf.

[4] Neil Gough, "What Trade Overhaul?" *South China Morning Post*, December 10, 2011.

[5] Yajie Li, "Xi Jinping: Strategic Emerging Industries Will Decide the Future Commanding Heights of the Economy (习近平: 战略性新兴产业决定未来经济发展制高点)," *Xinhua News*, April 10, 2011. http://finance.eastmoney.com/news/1344,20110410129227138.html.

[6] Yigong Shi and Yi Rao, "China's Research Culture," *Science Magazine*, Vol. 329, no. 5996 (September 3, 2010): 1128.

[7] "Capital Controversy," *The Economist*, April 14, 2012. http://www.economist.com/node/21552555.

[8] "Quotable Quotes from Hu Jintao's Speech on CPC's 90th Founding Anniversary," Xinhua News, July 1, 2011. http://news.xinhuanet.com/english2010/china/2011-07/01/c_13960798.htm.

[9] "Executive Profile: China Everbright International Limited: Li Xueming," *Bloomberg News*, http://investing.businessweek.com/research/stocks/people/.

[10] "China Murder Suspect's Sisters Ran $126 Million Empire," Bloomberg, April 14, 2012. http://www.bloomberg.com/news/2012-04-13/china-murder-suspect-s-sisters-ran-126-million-business-empire.html.

[11] "State-Owned Firms Pledge to Spend 350 Billion Yuan in Chongqing," *Economic Observer*, June 9, 2012. http://www.eeo.com.cn/ens/2012/0521/226827.shtml.

[12] Michael Forsythe, "The Chinese Communist Party's Capitalist Elite," *Bloomberg News*, March 1, 2012. http://www.businessweek.com/articles/2012-03-01/the-chinese-communist-partys-capitalist-elite.

[13] Feng Wang, "China's Population Destiny: The Looming Crisis," Brookings-Tsinghua Center, February 6, 2011. http://www.brookings.edu/research/articles/2010/09/china-population-wang.

[14] Liu, "The Basic Logic behind the 12th Five-Year Plan," 12.

[15] Author's interview with trade attorney who requested anonymity.

[16] Author's interview with company executive who requested anonymity.

[17] "The Government Admits the Implementation of the New 36 Clauses to Encourage Private Investment Is Not Ideal (政府承认鼓励民间投资"新36条"推进不理想)," *Caixin News*, February 22, 2012. http://economy.caixin.com/2012-02-22/100359326.html.

[18] "Detailed Implementation Plans for New 36 Clauses Released, Favorable Policies for Private Investments (新36条实施细则密集出台 民间资本迎政策"暖春)," *China News*, May 28, 2012. http://finance.chinanews.com/cj/2012/05-28/3919086.shtml.

[19] Kevin Yao, "Analysis: China's New Privatization Plan Faces Push-back Risk," *Reuters*, May 24, 2012. http://www.reuters.com/article/2012/05/24/us-china-economy-investment-id USBRE84N1N220120524

[20] "China's Top Paper Defends Grip of State Firms," *Reuters*, June 1, 2012. http://www.reuters.com/article/2012/06/01/us-china-economy-state-idUSBRE85004Y20120601.

[21] Barry Naughton, *The Chinese Economy: Transitions and Growth* (Cambridge: The MIT Press, 2006), 300.

[22] Naughton, *The Chinese Economy*, 274–275.

[23] Naughton, "Profiting the SASAC Way," *China Economics Quarterly* 12 (June 2008): 19.

[24] "China Adopts the Chaebol," *The Economist*, June 5, 1997. http://www.economist.com/node/90635.

[25] Carl Walter and Fraser J.T. Howie, *Red Capitalism: The Fragile Financial Foundation of China's Extraordinary Rise*, (John Wiley & Sons: February 2011), 11.

[26] "China Adopts the Chaebol," *The Economist*.

[27] Barry Naughton, *The Chinese Economy*, 105–106.

[28] Barry Naughton, "Profiting the SASAC Way," 20–21.

[29] USCC, "An Analysis of State-owned Enterprises and State Capitalism in China," 8.

[30] USCC, "An Analysis of State-owned Enterprises and State Capitalism in China," 8.

[31] "Definitions: Industry," National Bureau of Statistics of China, last modified May 17, 2002. http://www.stats.gov.cn/english/classificationsmethods/definitions/t20020517_402 787574.htm.

[32] "NBS Held Press Conference to Announce to Industries about Readjustment in Statistical Standards," National Bureau of Statistics of China, (国家统计局召开 通气会通报工业和投资统计起点标准调整)," last modified March 8, 2011. http://www.stats.gov.cn/tjdt/gjtjjdt/t20110308_402709134.htm.

[33] USCC, "An Analysis of State-owned Enterprises and State Capitalism in China," 8.

[34] "Li Rongrong: Zhu Rongji Is My Role Model and Putin Is My Idol (李荣融 : 以朱镕基为榜样 以普京为偶像)," Xinhua News, September 8, 2010. http://finance.qq.com/a/20100908/004556.htm.

[35] USCC, "An Analysis of State-owned Enterprises and State Capitalism in China," 21.

[36] "Li Rongrong: Zhu Rongji Is My Role Model and Putin is My Idol," Xinhua News.

[37] USCC, "An Analysis of State-owned Enterprises and State Capitalism in China," 35–41.

[38] Hongliang Zheng and Yang Yang, "Chinese Private Sector Development in the Past 30 Years: Retrospect and Prospect," Discussion Paper 45, March 2009, China Policy Institute, Nottingham University, 10. http://www.nottingham.ac.uk/cpi/documents/discussion-papers/discussion-paper-45-hongliang-zheng-chinese-private-sector.pdf.

[39] Hongliang Zheng and Yang Yang, "Chinese Private Sector Development in the Past 30 Years."

[40] Richard McGregor, The Party: The Secret World of China's Communist Rulers, (Harper Collins, Inc. 2010), 202–205.

[41] Research team's interview with subject who requested anonymity.

[42] "Wang Shi: Vanke's Two Red Hats (王石: 万科的两项红帽子)," 21st Century Business Herald, December 30, 2008. http://bj.house.sina.com.cn/news/2008-12-30/0912293408.html.

[43] "The Nature, Performance and Reform of State-owned Enterprises," Unirule Institute of Economics, June 16, 2011, Beijing, 243.

[44] "SASAC Shows Central SOEs Profitability Ranking in 2010, Three Oil Companies Are among Top-four (国资委亮出2010年央企净利润排行 "三桶油" 位列前四)," People.com.cn, October 22, 2011. SASAC only released financial data of 102 central SOEs. In 2010, there were 125 central SOEs in total. http://ccnews.people.com.cn/GB/15982174.html.

[45] Naughton, "Profiting the SASAC Way," 21–22.

[46] Cheng Li, "China's Midterm Jockeying: Gearing Up for 2012 (Part 4: Top Leaders of Major State-Owned Enterprises)," China Leadership Monitor 34 (February

11, 2011), Stanford University: Hoover Institution, 13. http://www.hoover.org/publications/china-leadership-monitor/article/68001.

⁴⁷ Jim O'Connell, "The Year of the Metal Rabbit: Antitrust Enforcement in China in 2011," *Antitrust,* Vol. 26 No. 2, Spring 2012: 65. http://www.cov.com/files/Publication/

⁴⁸ O'Connell, "The Year of the Metal Rabbit."

⁴⁹ David Barboza, "Entrepreneur's Rival in China: The State," *New York Times,* December 7, 2011. http://www.nytimes.com/2011/12/08/business/an-entrepeneurs-rival-in-china-the-state.html?pagewanted=all.

⁵⁰ Downs & Meidan, "Business and Politics in China," 121.

⁵¹ Barry Naughton, "SASAC and Rising Corporate Power in China," *China Leadership Monitor,* 24 (March 12, 2008), Stanford University: Hoover Institution, 5. http://media.hoover.org/sites/default/files/documents/CLM24BN.pdf.

⁵² Adam Segal, "China's Innovation Wall: Beijing's Push for Foreign Technology," *Foreign Affairs,* September 28, 2010. http://www.foreignaffairs.com/articles/66753/adam-segal/chinas-innovation-wall.

⁵³ "PRC Government Actions to Meet Bilateral Commitments on Indigenous Innovation and Government Procurement," The US–China Business Council (USCBC), October 12, 2011. https://www.uschina.org/public/documents/2011/10/procurement-delink-actions.pdf.

⁵⁴ State Council General Office Cable, "Notification Regarding Deepening the Work for Removal of Documents Linking Innovation Policies to Government Procurement Incentives," November 17, 2011.

⁵⁵ Research team's interview with subject who requested anonymity.

⁵⁶ Chris Buckley, "China Confirms $1.7 Trillion Spending Plan: US," *Reuters,* November 21, 2011. http://www.reuters.com/article/2011/11/21/us-china-us-idUSTRE7AK0MT20111121.

⁵⁷ Author's interview with subject who requested anonymity.

⁵⁸ "Public Procurement in China: European Business Experiences Competing for Public Contracts in China," European Union Chamber of Commerce in China (EUCCC), April, 2011, 15. http://www.europeanchamber.com.cn/images/documents/marketing_department/beijing/publications/2011/PP%20Study%20EN%20Final_0421.pdf.

⁵⁹ "China's ZUC 4G LTE Encryption Algorithm Background & Implications for Foreign Industry," Information Technology Industry Council, United States Information Technology Office, and Telecommunications Industry Association, January 23, 2012.

⁶⁰ "China's ZUC 4G LTE Encryption Algorithm."

61 Author and research team interviews with industry experts.

62 Research team's interview with subject who requested anonymity.

63 Junhua Zhang, "Network Convergence and Bureaucratic Turf Wars," in *China and the Internet: Politics of the Digital Leap Forward*, ed. Christopher Hughes and Gudrun Wacker. (New York: Routledge, 2003), 83.

64 "The Powers That Be: The Black Hole of Regulation, Censorship and Money-making," *China Economic Review,* December 1, 2011. http://www.chinaeconomicreview.com/content/powers-be-black-hole-regulation-censorship-money-making.

65 Hejuan Zhao, "IPTV Statistic Slows Network Integration Project," *Century Weekly Magazine*, April 6, 2010. http://english.caixin.com/2010-06-04/100150005.html.

66 Hejuan Zhao, "IPTV Statistic Slows Network Integration Project."

67 "IPTV in China: Only 14 Million Subscribers after Eight Years," *China Times,* March 13, 2012. http://www.thechinatimes.com/online/2012/03/2696.html.

68 Hejuan Zhao, "Disputes Sound Media Integration Death Knell," *Century Weekly Magazine,* April 12, 2011. http://english.caixin.com/2011-04-12/100247201.html.

69 "The 4th Cloud Computing China Congress," March 12, 2012. http://www.cloudcomputingchina.org/index.html.

70 "Press Release: Asia's First 'Cloud Readiness Index,'" Asia Cloud Computing Association, September 7, 2011. http://www.asiacloud.org/index.php/news/press-release-asias-first-cloud-readiness-index.

71 "$103 Million Injected into Cloud Computing Research," *China Daily*, November 25, 2011. http://www.chinadaily.com.cn/china/2011-11/25/content_14165265.htm.

72 "Lockout: How a New Wave of Trade Protectionism Is Spreading through the World's Fastest-Growing IT Markets—and What to Do About It," Business Software Alliance, June 2012. http://www.bsa.org/~/media/Files/Policy/Trade/BSA_Market%20Access_Report_FINAL_WEB_062012.ashx

73 Research team's interview with subject who requested anonymity.

74 Shaohua Gao, "In the Name of Cloud Computing Some Enterprises Invest in Real Estate (部分企业以云计算为名行圈地之实)," *Economic Information*, December 6, 2011. http://dz.jjckb.cn/www/pages/webpage2009/html/2011-12/06/content_37738.htm?div=-1.

75 Shaohua Gao, "In the Name of Cloud Computing Some Enterprises Invest in Real Estate."

[76] Wayne, Arnold, "Regulations and Security Concerns Hinder Asia's Move to Cloud Computing," *New York Times,* October 10, 2010. http://www.nytimes.com/2010/10/11/technology/11cloudasia.html.

[77] The World Bank and the State Council Development Research Center of the People's Republic of China, "China 2030: Building a Modern, Harmonious, and Creative High-Income Society," 6. http://www.worldbank.org/content/dam/Worldbank/document/China-2030-complete.pdf.

[78] Research team's interview with subject who requested anonymity.

[79] James T. Areddy and Norihiko Shirouzu, "China Bullet Trains Trip on Technology," *Wall Street Journal,* October 3, 2011. http://online.wsj.com/article/SB10001424053111904353504576568983658561372.html.

[80] Jamil Anderlini and Mure Dickie, "China: A Future on Track," *Financial Times,* September 23, 2010. http://www.ft.com/cms/s/0/2b843e4c-c745-11df-aeb1-00144feab49a.html#axzz1vggpRFjE.

[81] Kevin Jianjun Tu, "A Warning for China's Nuclear Sector," *China Dialogue,* August 10, 2011. http://www.chinadialogue.net/article/show/single/en/4458.

[82] Ning Yu, "Closer Look: The Rail Ministry's Staggering Debt," *Caixin,* July 26, 2011. http://english.caing.com/2011-07-26/100284096.html.

[83] Ning Yu, Boling Zhang, Haili Cao, Heyan Wang and Dongmei Liang, "Fast Track Wreck for Rail Minister's Circle," *Century Weekly Magazine,* March 2, 2011. http://english.caixin.com/2011-03-02/100231179.html.

[84] Ian Johnson, "In China, Part of Railway Collapses Despite Test Runs," *New York Times*, March 12, 2012. http://www.nytimes.com/2012/03/13/world/asia/tested-section-of-new-high-speed-rail-track-disintegrates-in-china.html.

[85] Ellen Nakashima, "In a World of Cybertheft, US Names China, Russia as Main Culprits." *Washington Post,* November 3, 2011. http://www.washingtonpost.com/world/national-security/us-cyber-espionage-report-names-china-and-russia-as-main-culprits/2011/11/02/gIQAF5fRiM_story.html.

[86] Research team's interview with subject who requested anonymity.

[87] "Foreign Spies Stealing US Economic Secrets in Cyberspace," United States Office of The National Counterintelligence Executive, October 2011, executive summary, i. http://www.ncix.gov/publications/reports/fecie_all/Foreign_Economic_Collection_2011.pdf.

[88] Nicole Perlroth, "Traveling Light in a Time of Digital Thievery," *New York Times,* Feb 10, 2012.

http://www.nytimes.com/2012/02/11/technology/electronic-security-a-worry-in-an-age-of-digital-espionage.html?pagewanted=all.

[89] Michael Riley and John Walcott, "China-Based Hacking of 760 Companies Shows Cyber Cold War," *Bloomberg News*, December 14, 2011. http://www.bloomberg.com/news/2011-12-13/china-based-hacking-of-760-companies-reflects-undeclared-global-cyber-war.html.

90 Adam Segal, "Innovation, Espionage and Chinese Technology Policy." Council on Foreign Relations, April 15, 2011, 2. http://foreignaffairs.house.gov/112/Seg041511.pdf.

[91] Riley and Walcott, "China-Based Hacking of 760 Companies Shows Cyber Cold War."

[92] Riley and Walcott, "China-Based Hacking of 760 Companies Shows Cyber Cold War."

[93] "Foreign Spies Stealing US Economic Secrets," The National Counterintelligence Executive, 5.

[94] Justin Scheck, "China Secrets Case Yields Indictment," *Wall Street Journal*, February 9, 2012. http://online.wsj.com/article/SB10001424052970203315804577211463864126278.html.

[95] Scheck, "China Secrets Case Yields Indictment."

[96] Scheck, Justin and Evan Perez. "FBI Traces Trail of Spy Ring to China," *Wall Street Journal*, March 10, 2012. http://online.wsj.com/article/SB10001424052970203961204577266892884130620.html.

[97] Leslie Hook, "AMSC to Sue Sinovel in Beijing Court," *Financial Times*, November 4, 2011. http://www.ft.com/cms/s/0/b5e190c8-05db-11e1-a079-00144feabdc0.html#axzz1vmHI8wBp.

[98] Hook, "AMSC to Sue Sinovel in Beijing Court."

[99] Herman K. Trabish, "Can AMSC Recover from Alleged IP Theft by China's Biggest Wind Company." *Greentechmedia*, November 14, 2011. http://www.greentechmedia.com/articles/read/Can-AMSC-Recover-From-Alleged-IP-Theft-by-Chinas-Biggest-Wind-Company/

[100] Michael A. Riley and Ashlee Vance, "China Corporate Espionage Boom Knocks Wind Out of US Companies," *Bloomberg News*, March 16, 2012. http://www.bloomberg.com/news/2012-03-15/china-corporate-espionage-boom-knocks-wind-out-of-u-s-companies.html.

[101] Riley and Vance, "China Corporate Espionage Boom Knocks Wind Out of US Companies."

[102] Riley and Vance, "China Corporate Espionage Boom Knocks Wind Out of US Companies."

[103] As of 2010, there were 90 listed on the New York Stock Exchange, 145 on Nasdaq, 10 on American Stock Exchange, 123 on Hong Kong H Share, 35 on Hong Kong Growth Enterprise Market, 125 on Singapore Stock Exchange, and 5 on London Stock Exchange, or in total: 534.

[104] "Global Fortune 500 2012: By Location," *CNN Money*, July 2012. http://money.cnn.com/magazines/fortune/global500/2012/countries/China.html. The Global Fortune 500 lists 73 companies from China, including four in Hong Kong.

[105] Research team's interview with subject who requested anonymity.

[106] Li-Wen Lin and Curtis J. Milhaupt, "We Are the (National) Champions: Understanding the Mechanisms of State Capitalism," Columbia University School of Law, Working Paper No. 409, (November 2011). 46.

[107] USCC, "An Analysis of State-owned Enterprises and State Capitalism in China," 78.

[108] "Our Company," China Petroleum & Chemical Corporation (Sinopec), accessed on April 10, 2012. http://english.sinopec.com/about_sinopec/our_company/6as7tuvr.shtml.

[109] "Announcement Regarding the Increased Shareholdings in Sinopec Corp. By the Controlling Shareholder," Sinopec," April 10, 2012. http://english.sinopec.com/media_center/announcements/20120110/download/2012011003.pdf.

[110] Micah Springut, Stephen Schlaikjer, and David Chen (CENTRA Technology Inc.), "China's Program for Science and Technology Modernization: Implications for American Competitiveness," US-China Economic and Security Review Commission (January 2011), 113. http://www.uscc.gov/researchpapers/2011/USCC_REPORT_China's_Program_for_Science_and_Technology_Modernization.pdf.

[111] Michael Mecham and Joseph C Anselmo, "Aviation's Learnaholics," *Aviation Week & Space Technology*, (April/May, 2011): 44.

[112] David Pierson, "China to Unveil Its Own Large Jetliner," *Los Angeles Times*, November 13, 2010. http://articles.latimes.com/2010/nov/13/business/la-fi-china-jetliner-20101113.

[113] "235 Orders for China's Homegrown C919 Passenger Plane," *Xinhua News*, March 5, 2012, http://news.xinhuanet.com/english/china/2012-03/05/c_131448164.htm.

[114] Walter and Howie, *Red Capitalism*.

[115] Freshfields Bruckhaus Deringer, "Briefing: The Amended State Secret Law," July 2010. http://www.freshfields.com/publications/pdfs/2010/July10/28487.pdf.

[116] Company Website of China High Precision, "News Center: "Congratulations to the Successful Launch of Shenzhou Spaceship No. 8," China High Precision company website, November 9, 2011.

http://www.chpag.net/news_detail/newsId=410655f0-61b8-4a66-8561-2f18c203b5f1.html

[117] Paul Gillis, "State Secret and Auditing," *China Accounting Blog*, November 3, 2011.
http://www.chinaaccountingblog.com/weblog/state-secrets-and-auditing.html

[118] China High Precision Automation Group, "Clarification Announcement in Respect of Annual Results for the Year Ended June 30, 2011," 2.
http://chpag.todayir.com/attachment/2011102718170200129604_en.pdf.

[119] "Longtop Financial Fraud Investigation Reaches 'Final Step,'" *Business Insider*, August 30, 2011.
http://articles.businessinsider.com/2011-08-30/markets/30065320_1_sec-enforcement-chinese-firms-sec-and.

[120] Stanley Lubman, "Unpacking the Law around the Chinese Reverse Takeover Mess," *Wall Street Journal*, January 24, 2012.
http://blogs.wsj.com/chinarealtime/2012/01/24/unpacking-the-law-around-the-chinese-reverse-takeover-mess/.

[121] Jesse Hamilton, "US Regulators Push Chinese to Resume Auditor-inspection Talks," *Bloomberg BusinessWeek*,
http://www.businessweek.com/news/2011-12-01/u-s-regulators-push-chinese-to-resume-auditor-inspection-talks.html.

[122] Jesse Hamilton, "US Regulators Push Chinese to Resume Auditor-inspection Talks."

[123] Rachel Armstrong, "Big Four Auditors Brace for Big Changes in China," Reuters, February 28, 2012.
http://www.reuters.com/article/2012/02/28/us-china-accounting-idUSTRE81R07V20120228.

[124] Paul Gillis, "Big Four in China," *China Accounting Blog*, February 29, 2012.
http://chinaaccountingblog.com/weblog/big-four-in-china.html.

[125] "Risks Loom as China Orders Big 4 Auditors to Go Local," Reuters, May 10, 2012.
http://www.reuters.com/article/2012/05/10/china-auditors-risks-idUSL1E8GAFIM20120510.

[126] "Muddy Waters Stigma Means $1 Billion Cost to Exit US," *Bloomberg News*, July 10, 2012.
http://www.businessweek.com/news/2012-07-10/muddy-waters-stigma-means-1-billion-cost-to-exit-u-dot-s-dot.

[127] USCC, "An Analysis of State-owned Enterprises and State Capitalism in China," 52.

[128] Walter and Howie, *Red Capitalism*.

[129] Walter and Howie, *Red Capitalism*.

[130] Cheng Li, "China's Midterm Jockeying," 24.

[131] Diana Farrell, et al., "Putting China's Capital to Work: The Real Value of Financial System Reform," McKinsey Global Institute, May 2006, 61. http://www.mckinsey.com/Insights/MGI/Research/Financial_Markets/Putting_Chinas_capital_to_work.

[132] "Policy Brief: Economic Survey of China." Paris: Organization for Economic Cooperation and Development, 2005, 3. http://www.oecd.org/dataoecd/10/25/35294862.pdf.

[133] Farrell, et al., "Putting China's Capital to Work," 9.

[134] Walter and Howie, *Red Capitalism*.

[135] Lin and Milhaupt, "We Are the (National) Champions," 56.

[136] World Bank-DRC, "China 2030," 133.

[137] "What Does China's Wen Mean When He Says Break Bank Monopoly?" *Reuters*, April 4, 2012. http://www.reuters.com/article/2012/04/04/us-china-banks-wen-idUSBRE83308T20120404.

[138] "Closer Look: Policies to Promote Private Investment Just Symbolic," *Caixin Online*, June 12, 2012. http://english.caixin.com/2012-06-12/100399816.html.

[139] Walter and Howie, *Red Capitalism*, 75.

[140] Lin and Milhaupt, "We Are the (National) Champions," 46.

[141] Lin and Milhaupt, "We Are the (National) Champions," 56.

[142] Unirule, "The Nature, Performance and Reform of State-owned Enterprises," 34.

[143] USCC, "An Analysis of State-owned Enterprises and State Capitalism in China," 6.

[144] Research team's interview with subject who requested anonymity.

[145] "SASAC: Push for Centralized Administration of Local SASACs (国资委：推动地方经营性国资集中统一监管)," *The Securities Journal*, August 25, 2011. http://www.cbex.com.cn/article//jyyhq/llqy/201108/20110800032767.shtml.

[146] Lin and Milhaupt, "We Are the (National) Champions," 42.

[147] Downs & Meidan, "Business and Politics in China."

[148] Lin and Milhaupt, "We Are the (National) Champions," 27-28.

[149] Lin and Milhaupt, "We Are the (National) Champions," 45.

[150] McGregor, *The Party*, 72.

[151] Lin and Milhaupt, "We Are the (National) Champions," 38.

[152] "The Telecoms Reshuffle: More Harm than Good," *Caijing Magazine*, November 15, 2004. http://english.caijing.com.cn/2004-11-15/100013841.html.

[153] Erica Downs & Michal Meidan, "Business and Politics in China: The Oil Executive Reshuffle of 2011," World Security Institute, *China Security* Issue 19 (2011), 3. http://www.chinasecurity.us/index.php?option=com_content&view=article&id=489&Itemid=8.

[154] Cheng Li, "China's Midterm Jockeying," 1.

[155] Cheng Li, "China's Midterm Jockeying," 1.

[156] "The 12th Five-Year Plan Speeds up 'Going Out' Strategy, SOEs' Overseas Expansion Has Weaknesses ("十二五"走出去战略提速 央企海外扩张存短板和软肋)," *Caixun*, May 10, 2011.
http://economy.caixun.com/content/20110510/NEO2lbh7.html.

[157] Derek Scissors, "Chinese Outward Investment: Slower Growth in 2011," *Heritage Foundation*, January 9, 2012.
http://www.heritage.org/research/reports/2012/01/chinese-investment-slower-growth-in-china-foreign-investments-in-2011.

[158] Yangyong Chen, "The Formation and Significance of Jiang Zemin 'Going Out' Strategy (江泽民"走出去"战略的形成及其重要意义)," *The Communist Party of China*, November 10, 2008.
http://theory.people.com.cn/GB/40557/138172/138202/8311431.html.

[159] Antoaneta Bezlova, "'Win-win' deals at China-Africa summit," Asia Times Online, November 8, 2006.
http://www.atimes.com/atimes/China_Business/HK08Cb01.html.

[160] "GOIL, Sino Hydro Energy Sign Pact," *Modern Ghana*, June 23, 2008.
http://www.modernghana.com/news/171156/1/goil-sino-hydro-energy-sign-pact.html.

[161] David Shinn, "Africa: China's Growing Role in Africa—Implications for US Policy," Senate Committee on Foreign Relations Subcommittee on African Affairs, United States Congress, November 1, 2011.
http://allafrica.com/stories/201111021230.html.

[162] Christopher Alessi and Stephanie Hanson, "Expanding China-Africa Oil Ties," Council on Foreign Relations, February 8, 2012.
http://www.cfr.org/china/expanding-china-africa-oil-ties/p9557.

[163] Nicolas Bariyo, "Chinese-Owned Miner in Zambia Fires 1,000 Striking Workers," *Wall Street Journal*, October 21, 2011.
http://online.wsj.com/article/SB10001424052970204618704576642392413811456.html.

[164] "Zambian Miners Kill Chinese Manager During Pay Protest," BBC News, August 5, 2012.
http://www.bbc.co.uk/news/world-africa-19135435

[165] Howard W. French, "In Africa, an Election Reveals Skepticism of Chinese Involvement," *The Atlantic*, September 29, 2011.
http://www.theatlantic.com/international/archive/2011/09/in-africa-an-election-reveals-skepticism-of-chinese-involvement/245832/.

[166] Wei Han and Hu Shen, "Animal Instinct and China's African Odyssey, *Caixin Online*, April 2012.
http://english.caixin.com/2012-04-01/100375791.html.

[167] Robyn Dixon, "China offers Africa $20 billion in loans, promising a new approach," *Los Angeles Times,* July 19, 2012. http://latimesblogs.latimes.com/world_now/2012/07/china-africa-20-billion-in-loans.html.

[168] Francois Godement and Jonas Parello-Plesner, "The Scramble for Europe," European Council on Foreign Relations Policy Brief, July, 2011, 5. http://www.ecfr.eu/page/-/ECFR37_Scramble_For_Europe_AW_v4.pdf.

[169] "Chinese Firms Buy into Europe," EU Business, February 19, 2012. http://www.eubusiness.com/news-eu/china-auto.fah.

[170] Ting Xu, "Destination Unknown: Investment in China's 'Go out' Policy," *China Brief, Jamestown Foundation: China Brief,* Vol. 11, Issue 17, September 16, 2011. http://www.jamestown.org/programs/chinabrief/single/?tx_ttnews%5Btt_news%5D=38413&cHash=e26e023d998752150d820e70ddc9088b.

[171] Chris V. Nicholson, "Cnooc Adds to Chesapeake Energy Stake," *New York Times,* January 31, 2011. http://dealbook.nytimes.com/2011/01/31/cnooc-takes-further-chesapeake-stake/

[172] Angel Gonzelez and Ryan Dezember, "Sinopec Enters US Shale," *Wall Street Journal*, January 4, 2012. http://online.wsj.com/article/SB1000142405297020355030457713849319232550 0.html.

[173] Wan Xu and Don Durfee, "China's State Grid in Talks to Buy AES' US Wind Assets: Sources," *Reuters*, February 27, 2012. http://www.reuters.com/article/2012/02/27/us-aes-chinastategrid-wind-idUS-TRE81Q0QL20120227.

[174] "The US Approved of China's State-owned Bank's Acquisition in the US for the First Time," *Xinhua News,* May 14, 2012. http://www.e521.com/news/hwxw/264350.shtml.

[175] Michael Cieply, "Deal Expands Chinese Influence on Hollywood," *New York Times*, May 20, 2012. http://www.nytimes.com/2012/05/21/business/global/amc-theater-deal-links-china-to-hollywood.html.

[176] Roger Vincent, "Shenzhen New World Group Buys Sheraton Universal Hotel," *Los Angeles Times*, January 6, 2011. http://articles.latimes.com/2011/jan/06/business/la-fi-sheraton-20110106.

[177] Daniel H. Rosen and Thilo Hanemann, "An American Open Door? Maximizing the Benefits of Chinese Foreign Direct Investment," *Asia Society,* May 2011, 16. http://asiasociety.org/files/pdf/AnAmericanOpenDoor_FINAL.pdf.

[178] Jamil Anderlini, "Visa Blocked in China after UnionPay Dispute," *Financial Times*, September 16, 2010. http://www.ft.com/intl/cms/s/0/890f6152-c19d-11df-8e03-00144feab49a.html#axzz1vmHI8wBp.

[179] "Press Release: China UnionPay and American Express to Explore Opportunities Inside and Outside China," American Express, November 18, 2010. http://about.americanexpress.com/news/pr/2010/unionpay.aspx.

[180] "Certain Measures Affecting Electronic Payment Services," World Trade Organization, July 2012. http://www.wto.org/english/tratop_e/dispu_e/cases_e/ds413_e.htm

[181] James Politi, "WTO Rules Against China on Payment Cards," *Financial Times,* July 16, 2012. http://www.ft.com/intl/cms/s/0/fd631de4-cf67-11e1-a1d2-00144feabdc0. html#axzz20ygbAUYX.

[182] Author's interview with banker who requested anonymity.

[183] "Research Report on Chinese Bank Card Market, 2010-2011," China Research and Intelligence, September 8, 2010. http://www.researchandmarkets.com/reportinfo.asp?report_id=1343445&t=t.

[184] Author's interview with banker who requested anonymity.

[185] Geoff Dyer, Jamil Anderlini, and Henry Sender, "China's Lending Hits New Heights," *Financial Times*, January 17, 2011. http://www.ft.com/intl/cms/s/0/488c60f4-2281-11e0-b6a2-00144feab49a.html #axzz23lw3hYGw.

[186] Author's interview with trade attorney who requested anonymity.

[187] Baldwin, "Failure of the WTO Ministerial Conference at Cancun," 8.

[188] "How the negotiations are organized," World Trade Organization, http://www.wto.org/english/tratop_e/dda_e/work_organi_e.htm.

[189] "World Trade Organization, Annual Report 2012," Chapter 3, 3. http://www.wto.org/english/res_e/booksp_e/anrep_e/anrep12_chap3_e.pdf.

[190] Aaditya Mattoo and Arvind Subramanian, "China and the World Trading System," the World Bank Development Research Group Trade and Integration Team, December 2011.

[191] Author's interview with attorney who requested anonymity.

[192] "Trade Pact Complicates Prospects for Asia," *China Daily.* http://www.chinadaily.com.cn/cndy/2011-11/11/content_14075918.htm.

[193] United States Trade Representative (USTR), "2011 Report to Congress on China's WTO Compliance," December 2011, 2. http://www.ustr.gov/webfm_send/3189.

[194] USTR, "2011 Report to Congress on China's WTO Compliance," 2.

[195] Research team's interview with subject who requested anonymity.

[196] Business Europe, "Rising to the China Challenge," October 2011. http://www.businesseurope.eu/Content/default.asp?pageid=568&docid= 29298

[197] Matthew Dalton, "Europe Weighs Trade Probes amid Beijing Threats," *Wall Street Journal*, March 22, 2012.

http://online.wsj.com/article/SB100014240527023038129045772976039478833
14.html.

[198] Daniel Michaels, "China Envoy Backs Shunning of Airbus," *Wall Street Journal,* March 9, 2012.
http://online.wsj.com/article/SB100014240529702047818045772713127756631
08.html

[199] Michael Punke, "On the China Transitional Review of the Protocol of Accession to the WTO Agreement," Office of the United States Trade Representative, November 30, 2011.
http://www.ustr.gov/about-us/press-office/press-releases/2011/november/remarks-united-states-ambassador-world-trade-orga.

[200] Andrew H. Card, et al., "US Trade and Investment Policy," Council on Foreign Relations Task Force Report No. 67, September 2011, 52.
http://www.cfr.org/trade/us-trade-investment-policy/p25737.

[201] Mattoo and Subramanian, "China and the World Trading System," 14.

[202] Ken Jarrett and Amy Wendholt, "Transferring Technology to Transform China—Is It Worth It?" *China Business Review,* March–April 2010, 23.

[203] "The China Greentech Initiative Report 2011," China Greentech Initiative, 79.
http://www.china-greentech.com/node/2826.

[204] "The China Greentech Initiative Report 2011," 75.

[205] "Of Metals and Market Forces," *The Economist,* February 4, 2012.
http://www.economist.com/node/21546013.

[206] Qi Zhang, Qingfen Ding, and Jing Fu, "Rare Earths Export Quota Unchanged," *China Daily,* July 15, 2011.
http://www.chinadaily.com.cn/bizchina/2011-07/15/content_12910072.htm.

[207] Keith Bradsher, "Supplies Squeezed, Rare Earth Prices Surge," *New York Times,* May 2, 2011.
http://www.nytimes.com/2011/05/03/business/03rare.html?_r=1&pagewanted=all.

[208] Xiao Yu and Eugene Tang, "China Considers Rare-Earth Reserve in Inner Mongolia," *Bloomberg News,* September 2, 2009.
http://www.bloomberg.com/apps/news?pid=newsarchive&sid=aEEImPZH6Gcs.

[209] "United States Challenges China's Export Restraints on Rare Earths," Office of the USTR, March 2012.
http://www.ustr.gov/about-us/press-office/press-releases/2012/march/united-states-challenges-china%E2%80%99s-export-restraints-r.

[210] Keith Bradsher, "In Victory for the West, WTO Orders China to Stop Export Taxes on Minerals," *New York Times,* January 30, 2012.
http://www.nytimes.com/2012/01/31/business/wto-orders-china-to-stop-export-taxes-on-minerals.html?_r=1&ref=rareearths&pagewanted=all.

[211] Keith Bradsher, "China Consolidates Grip on Rare Earth," *New York Times,*

September 15, 2011. http://www.nytimes.com/2011/09/16/business/global/china-consolidates-control-of-rare-earth-industry.html?pagewanted=all.

212 "China—Measures Affecting Imports of Automobile Parts," World Trade Organization. http://www.wto.org/english/tratop_e/dispu_e/cases_e/ds340_e.htm.

213 Card et al., "US Trade and Investment Policy," 51.

214 Card et al., "US Trade and Investment Policy," 53–54.

215 "Joint US-China Economic Track Fact Sheet- Fourth Meeting of the US China Strategic and Economic Dialogue (S&ED)." http://www.treasury.gov/press-center/press-releases/Pages/tg1567.aspx.

216 Author interviews with US officials and business leaders who requested anonymity.

217 "US–China Joint Commission on Commerce and Trade," Office of the USTR, October 2009. http://www.ustr.gov/about-us/press-office/fact-sheets/2009/october/us-china-joint-commission-commerce-and-trade.

218 "2011 US-China Joint Commission on Commerce and Trade Outcomes," Office of the USTR, November 2011. http://www.ustr.gov/about-us/press-office/fact-sheets/2011/november/2011-us-china-joint-commission-commerce-and-trade-ou.

219 Interviews with foreign automakers in China who requested anonymity.

220 "China's JCCT Commitments, 2004–11," USCBC, updated November 21, 2011. https://www.uschina.org/public/documents/2012/jcct_2004-2011.pdf.

221 Interview with foreign technology executive who requested anonymity.

222 "China's JCCT Commitments, 2004–11," USCBC.

223 Author and research team's interview with a government official who requested anonymity.

224 "Business Confidence Survey 2012: Despite strong growth optimism, regulatory concerns and rising costs are impacting upon European companies' investment plans," the European Union Chamber of Commerce in China, May 29, 2012. http://www.euccc.com.cn/en/press-releases/1619.

225 Author's interview with a trade attorney who requested anonymity.

226 John Lee, "China's Corporate Leninism," *American Interest*, May/June 2012. http://www.the-american-interest.com/article.cfm?piece=1231.

227 "Obama Presses China to Act Like 'Grown Up' Nation," *Reuters*, November 13, 2011. http://www.reuters.com/article/2011/11/14/us-apec-obama-china-idUSTRE7AD08420111114.

228 Zhong Sheng, "There is No Unchanging Rules of Game in the World

(世界上没有一成不变的游戏规则)," *People's Daily*, February 1, 2012. http://opinion.people.com.cn/GB/16985508.html.

[229] "Push to Privatize SOEs a Foreign Plot," *South China Morning Post*, April 11, 2012. http://www.scmp.com/portal/site/SCMP/menuitem.2af62ecb329d3d7733492d925 3a0a0a0/?vgnextoid=906533c51dc96310VgnVCM100000360a0a0aRCRD&ss= China&s=News. (Subscription required.)

[230] Dong Wang and Li Kan, "Eyeing the Crippled Hegemon: China's Grand Strategy Thinking in the Wake of the Global Financial Crisis," School of International Studies, Peking University, September 2010.

[231] Ha-Joon Chang, *Bad Samaritans: The Myth of Free Trade and the Secret History of Capitalism*, (Bloomsbury Press, 2008), 44-45.

[232] Chang, *Bad Samaritans*, 51.

[233] World Bank-DRC, "China 2030," 12.

[234] World Bank-DRC, "China 2030," 9.

[235] He Liu, "The Basic Logic behind the 12th Five-Year Plan," 13.

[236] "Hukou Reform: A Mid to Long Term Goal, Picking up Pace," Goldman Sachs Global Investment Research, February 10, 2011, 3. http://www.goldmansachs.com/our-thinking/global-economic-outlook/global-econ-outlook-pdfs/huroku-report.pdf.

[237] Megan K. Stack, "China Raising a Generation of Left-behind Children," *Los Angeles Times*, September 2010. http://articles.latimes.com/2010/sep/29/world/la-fg-china-left-behind-20100930.

[238] Liu, "The Basic Logic behind the 12th Five-Year Plan."

[239] Bonnie Glaser, "China's 11th Ambassadorial Conference Signals Continuity and Change in Foreign Policy," *Jamestown Foundation: China Brief*, Volume 9, Issue 22 (November 2009). http://www.jamestown.org/programs/chinabrief/single/?tx_ttnews%5Btt_news%5 D=35691&tx_ttnews%5BbackPid%5D=414&no_cache=1.

[240] Willy Lam, "Mixing Marxism and Capitalism: CCP Celebrates its 90th Birthday," *Jamestown Foundation: China Brief*, Volume 11, Issue 12 (July 1, 2011). http://www.jamestown.org/programs/chinabrief/single/?tx_ttnews%5Btt_news%5 D=38129&tx_ttnews%5BbackPid%5D=25&cHash=bb9aecdd5fa45f9d8486dca4f 2a4d908.

[241] Forsythe, "The Chinese Communist Party's Capitalist Elite."

[242] Minxin Pei, "China's Politics of the Economically Possible," *Project Syndicate*, March 16, 2012. http://www.project-syndicate.org/commentary/china-s-politics-of-the-economically-possible.